The Self-Help Way to Treat Colitis and

Other IBS Conditions

SECOND EDITION

De Lamar Gibbons, M.D., graduated from the George Washington University School of Medicine in 1969. He practiced in rural Utah and Idaho for twenty-five years. Later he served as Director of Clinical Research for the *Saturday Evening Post*. While there, he discovered the pivotal role of fructose intolerance in Crohn's disease and ulcerative colitis. He is the author of several books, and has been published in the *AMA News*, the *Journal of the American Medical Association*, *Emergency Medicine*, *Medical Tribune*, *Family Practice News*, and numerous other publications.

The Self-Help Way to Treat Colitis and Other IBS Conditions

SECOND EDITION

De Lamar Gibbons, M.D.

New York Chicago San Francisco Lisbon London Madrid Mexico City
Milan New Delhi San Juan Seoul Singapore Sydney Toronto

Library of Congress Cataloging-in-Publication Data

Gibbons, De Lamar.
    The Self-help way to treat colitis and other IBS conditions / De Lamar
Gibbons.—2nd ed.
        p.   cm.
    First ed. published under title: The self-help way to treat colitis and other IBS
disorders.
    Includes bibliographical references and index.
    ISBN 0-658-01217-7 (acid-free paper)
    1. Irritable colon—Diet therapy.   I. Gibbons, De Lamar. Self-help way to
treat colitis and other IBS disorders.   II. Title.

RC862.I77 G53   2001
616.3'42—dc21   2001029659

Reprinted by arrangement with De Lamar Gibbons, M.D.

6 7 8 9 10 11 12 13 14 15 16 17 18 19 20 21   FGR/FGR   0 9 8 7 6

ISBN-13: 978-0-658-01217-4
ISBN-10:   0-658-01217-7

Cover design by Laurie Young
Interior design by Robert S. Tinnon

McGraw-Hill books are available at special quantity discounts to use as premiums
and sales promotions, or for use in corporate training programs. For more
information, please write to the Director of Special Sales, Professional Publishing,
McGraw-Hill, Two Penn Plaza, New York, NY 10121-2298. Or contact your local
bookstore.

The purpose of this book is to educate. It is sold with the understanding that the
publisher and author shall have neither liability nor responsibility for any injury
caused or alleged to be caused directly or indirectly by the information contained in
this book. While every effort has been made to ensure its accuracy, the book's
contents should not be construed as medical advice. Each person's health needs
are unique. To obtain recommendations appropriate to your particular situation,
please consult a qualified health care provider.

This book was printed on acid-free paper.

Contents

Introduction

For the most part, patients are at the mercy of their physicians, whose education and experience provide knowledge about health and disease beyond that of the patient. Treatment is influenced by the doctor's knowledge and his attitude toward the patient and the patient's illness. A doctor who is not interested in irritable bowel syndrome (IBS) is not the one to go to for that problem. As the old adage goes, "If you want the very best medical care, find a doctor who has the same ailment as you have." In *The Self-Help Way to Treat Colitis and Other IBS Conditions*, I share my personal experience with this problem and, more important, the discovery I made while treating patients who suffer from irritable bowel diseases.

In the United States, there are so many diet experts and other "authorities" that the general public is unable to tell where to turn for sound advice. Those who should know the most about IBS and related disorders may, in fact, know very little. Too often, patients are told by gastroenterologists that "Diet has nothing to do with colitis" or to "Eat a good diet with lots of fruit and fiber." Unwittingly, these doctors' directives contain advice that could cause IBS.

Based on research I have conducted on myself and on my many afflicted patients, I have concluded that the missing piece of the IBS puzzle is intolerance to fructose. Fructose is the natural sugar found in honey and in sweet fruits and in recent years has been made synthetically from corn. Called "corn sweetener," it is an artificial honey. This sugar is twice as sweet as cane sugar and is less expensive to produce. It has been stealthily substituted for cane and beet sugars in our diets. It replaces those sugars in waffle syrup, ice cream, candy, soda pop, breakfast cereals, and numerous other foods. Most people are able to convert it into glucose and burn it for energy, but it is the most important factor for the majority of those with irritable bowel diseases. For example, the doubling of the incidence of Crohn's disease in the past twenty years closely parallels the increased use of fructose over the same period.

Fructose intolerance is an inherited metabolic inability to digest this sugar due to the absence of an enzyme in the digestive system. Afflicted individuals cannot turn fructose into glucose that can then be absorbed and metabolized for energy. The intake of excessive amounts of fructose may induce serious bowel irritation manifested as voluminous intestinal gas production, cramping, diarrhea, and rectal itching. The treatment is both obvious and simple: reduce fructose in the diet.

Each year, about twenty-three thousand Americans have their colons removed and colostomy openings made in their abdominal walls because of the damage done to the colon by colitis and related irritable bowel conditions. No one should have such surgery without first determining whether they are intolerant to fructose and the other everyday foods—including fiber—discussed in the following pages. Most people will respond to the dietary treatment outlined in this book, and surgery will be unnecessary when the offending food elements are eliminated.

Chapter 1

The IBS Diseases

Irritable bowel syndrome (IBS) is among the most common of all the chronic health disorders. It is estimated that 10 to 20 percent of the adult population has it. There is good reason to believe that a far greater number have mild forms of the affliction but attach little importance to the symptoms (or are perhaps too embarrassed to bring them to the attention of their doctors).

The number of people who have mild symptoms of irritable bowel disease (excessive intestinal gas formation; frequent bouts of diarrhea, abdominal cramps, or rectal itching; pencil- or ribbon-shaped stools; or blood or mucus in stools) is legion. Of those who seek medical help, most are given antispasmodic drugs, which do not treat the source of the problem but, like aspirin, give symptomatic relief only. For those treated in this manner, the problem goes on interminably.

Even in cases where symptoms are mild, the proper treatment of these conditions is important. Continued irritation leads to more serious ulceration of the bowel lining, malnutrition, anemia, weakness, diverticulosis, kidney stones, gallstones, and arthritis, and greatly increases one's chances of developing colon cancer.

Until now, the cause of these disorders has been a mystery and the treatment only palliative, and ofttimes barbaric. Not uncommonly, a colectomy (the surgical removal of the colon) and the establishment of a colostomy (an opening in the abdominal wall for fecal waste) is required to help unfortunate victims. All this for a disease that can be controlled by eliminating a few foods from the diet! The number of individuals requiring colostomies in the future could be greatly reduced by following the guidelines presented in this book.

Most irritable bowel disease can be successfully controlled by diet—but you must know the rules. The treatment suggested in this book is aimed at eliminating the causes of irritable bowel disease without relying on cortisone and other dangerous drug agents.

The Colitis Club research diet—the diet presented in this book—was first offered to readers of the *Saturday Evening Post* who were troubled with irritable bowel symptoms. Soon after, the mail began pouring in: more than thirty thousand people requested the diet. Included with the diet were survey forms to be filled out by individuals before they began the diet and after they had tried the diet for a month. The respondents overwhelmingly reported improvement in their condition while following the diet guidelines. The tabulation of the first 1,021 questionnaires showed that the diet had helped 90.4 percent of those with any of the irritable bowel conditions, including ulcerative colitis, Crohn's disease or regional enteritis, spastic colon, IBS, and other undiagnosed bowel problems. This confirmed my belief that diet plays a key role in the cause and treatment of these ailments.

The development of the diet can be traced to my own personal struggles with irritable bowel disease. At first I consulted the medical texts and current medical literature. The standard, accepted practices for treating the problem gave me minimal temporary relief. The dietary recommendations of gastroenterologists to "eat plenty of fruits and fiber, especially wheat bran" exacerbated the problem greatly. Like so many, I tried to identify various foods that seemed to worsen the symptoms. Unlike most others, however, I had the benefit of training in both medicine and chemistry. In listing the foods that caused symptoms, I was able to find common chemical elements. By identifying these common chemical entities in the offending foods, some of the pieces of the puzzle began to fall into place, and some of the rules one must follow to avoid dietary injury to the intestine became apparent.

The Anatomy of the Intestine

As food enters your mouth, your digestive system begins to work immediately as the salivary glands in your cheeks and under your tongue begin secreting digestive enzymes. From your mouth, the food enters a long tube called the esophagus that takes the food to the stomach. In the stomach the food is broken down by strong enzymes and hydrochloric acid. It then passes into the small intestine, a narrow tube about ten feet long covered on the outside by a thin membrane called the serosa (see Figure 1.1). This thin layer resembles plastic wrap. Beneath the serosa is a double layer of muscle. One layer encircles the intestine, the other runs longitudinally. The food is moved along the tube by rhythmic contraction and relaxation of these muscles.

Inside the muscular layers is the epithelium. This is a very complex layer. It has the dual role of producing digestive enzymes and absorbing food substances. This lining layer also acts as a protective barrier against unwanted chemicals and microorganisms entering the blood. (Damage done to the epithelium by irritable bowel disease, which impairs its protective function, may be the reason for the patient's increased susceptibility to cancer of the intestine.) The epithelial layer is devoid of nerves, and therefore serious damage often goes unnoticed.

The small intestine is the most important part of the digestive system as it is here that nutrients are absorbed

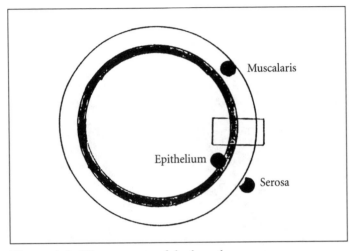

Figure 1.1: The anatomy of the bowel.

and passed to the various parts of the body. The food travels through the interior, which is lined with millions of tiny fingerlike projections called villi (see Figure 1.2A). These tiny structures greatly increase the reactive surface area of the intestine and are the digestive units or "machinery." Figure 1.2B reveals a network of blood vessels in the interior of a villus and a covering of tall columnar cells. A closer look at the columnar, or goblet, cells reveals the "brush border" covering the surface exposed to the food stream inside the intestine (see Figure 1.2C). The brush border is important because many of the digestive enzymes reside on the bristles of the brush.

The brush border is also quite fragile. It is easily damaged by infection or chemical insult and may be suddenly

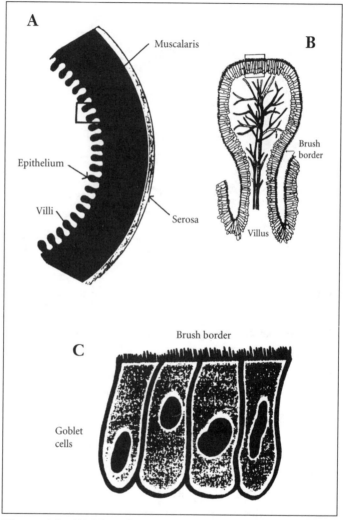

Figure 1.2: (A) Magnification of a small section of the epithelium in the small bowel; (B and C) magnification of a villus.

sloughed out. Diarrhea is usually associated with damage to the brush border. Its regrowth depends on the extent of the damage. Mild damage may be repaired in only a few days. Extensive injury may take months to restore. With the loss of the brush border, digestion is impaired and malabsorption or even malnutrition can occur.

In Crohn's disease and celiac-sprue, there is extensive damage to the villi that may progress to complete destruction. This results in large amounts of undigested food passing into the colon or large intestine where few nutrients are absorbed and billions of bacteria eat up what has not been digested. (No one digests and absorbs all one's food.) It is only when large amounts of undigested food ferment in the lower intestine that problems arise. What remains of the food after the bacterial action is mainly bacterial waste. This enters the last twelve inches of the bowel, which is called the rectum. Once waste is in the rectum, it stretches the walls of the bowel, and one gets the urge to pass a stool.

The Irritable Bowel Diseases

There are several of the irritable bowel diseases that are given different names and may or may not be separate entities. In many ways they interrelate and there is a question whether some of these are actually separate diseases or just different expressions of one or two pathologic conditions. For example, there is confusion about irritable bowel disease and IBS. Are they differing degrees of the same pathologic process or completely different entities? Or are they both mild expressions of ulcerative colitis or Crohn's disease? Are these latter conditions really different diseases or variations of the same? (Tests fail to clearly distinguish the difference between the two in one-third of cases.) The symptoms of the different conditions are often similar: intestinal gas formation, abdominal cramps, a tendency to pass diarrheal stools. In more severe cases there may be chronic diarrhea with bleeding from the bowels.

In his excellent article "IBD: Confirming Your Suspicions" in the May 1986 issue of *Diagnosis*, Dr. Howard M. Spiro, professor in the Department of Internal Medicine at the Yale University School of Medicine confirmed my suspicions with the following observation:

> Specialists argue among themselves whether ulcerative colitis and Crohn's colitis are different disorders. At Yale, we find it impossible to tell them apart by clincial, radiological, or even pathologic criteria in 25 to 35 percent of the patients.

This honesty is greatly appreciated and most reassuring to the doctors out in the trenches. We must not feel embarrassed if we are unable to distinguish between the two conditions.

Celiac-sprue seems to be a distinctly different entity from the above conditions. It has a different cause, supposedly being provoked by intolerance to gluten, the protein in wheat, barley, oats, and rye. (One wonders whether this intolerance is actually to the fiber in the grains, rather than to the accused protein.) Sprue relates to the above ailments as an intolerance to lactose, fructose, sorbitol, and mannitol that provokes the other maladies and is very common among celiac sufferers.

Many people suffer from these irritable bowel diseases without ever getting medical care or being diagnosed. I mentioned earlier in this chapter that 10 to 20 percent of American adults are estimated to have irritable bowel disease, but there is reason to suspect that the upper number is closer to 50 than 20 percent. Among those with mild disease, few even suspect that there is an abnormal process at play; they assume they are simply "gassy."

Ulcerative Colitis

Ulcerative colitis is probably the end stage of a severe expression of irritable bowel disease. It is manifested by chronic diarrhea (often bloody), large amounts of mucus in the stool, malnutrition with weight loss, anemia, hair loss, kidney stones, abdominal pain, and often arthritis, with some or all of these conditions being present (see Figure 1.3).

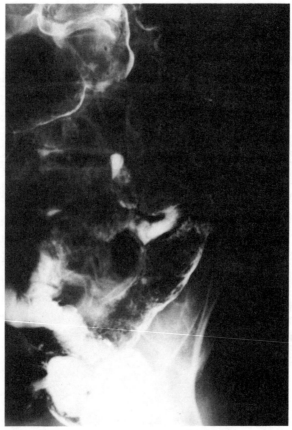

Figure 1.3: Ulcerative colitis. The motling or lacy appearance of the inside of the colon is due to the many small open sores or ulcers.

In severe attacks of the illness, the sufferer may have ten to twenty loose stools per day. These are accompanied by severe cramping pains that produce violent diarrhea with profuse gas production. The urge to defecate is immediate. High fever with severe episodes is not uncommon. When pain is noted, the ulcerated process has eroded through the lining layer of the bowel and is attacking the deeper muscular layers of the intestinal wall. (The mucous membrane lining the hollow of the intestine is largely devoid of sensory nerves, and early irritation is not likely to be painful. This is unfortunate because significant damage to the lining may be occurring without the patient being aware of the seriousness of the process.) Pain is an important warning that dangerous bowel disease is present. Mild ulcerative colitis is often diagnosed as IBS, spastic colitis, mucous colitis, or simply as colitis.

Severe ulcerative colitis is fraught with complications in addition to those mentioned above. The ulcers may perforate the colon and spill stool into the abdominal cavity, causing peritonitis. Perforations may also take the form of fistulas, or open passages, tunneling into the vagina, urinary bladder, other parts of the intestine, or even out through the skin. Stool may be passed through the vagina, in the urine, or out the abdominal wall. Other complications include severe liver damage of several kinds: primary biliary cirrhosis, fatty degeneration, and sclerosing angitis. All are potentially fatal.

The inflammatory process may paralyze the colon causing life-threatening toxic megacolon. Here the loss of the muscular action in the bowel wall results in a ballooning of the colon. The wall becomes dangerously thinned so rupture is likely with subsequent peritonitis and frequently death. Sudden, massive hemorrhage from the bowel may occur with grave consequences. Inflammation of the inner parts of the eyes has been associated with ulcerative colitis, specifically posterior uveitis. Children with significant ulcerative colitis suffer growth retardation.

Because of the serious effects of ulcerative colitis, a colostomy or ileostomy (bringing the bowel out through an opening in the abdominal wall) is the fate of many thousands of Americans annually. For some of those with arthritis induced by ulcerative colitis or Crohn's diease, colectomy and the formation of a colostomy may be helpful for the arthritis. For others, it may not be helpful. In any case, it is a terrible price to pay—especially for conditions potentially correctable by diet.

The diagnosis of ulcerative colitis is made by noting a typical pattern on a barium enema X ray or by direct visual inspection of the bowel lining by a proctoscopic or colonoscopic examination. Open ulcers on the lining are noted with tags, mucus lakes, detached folds called pseudo-polyps, and passes tunneled beneath the lining. Confirmation of these observations is made by taking biopsy specimens of the involved bowel.

The conventional treatment of ulcerative colitis has consisted of a lactose-free diet, one of the cortisone family of drugs for acute or severe disease, and sulfasalazine, a poorly absorbed sulfa. The cortisone reduces the inflammatory reaction in the bowel lining. The sulfa inhibits bacterial growth and reduces the alcohol and lactic acid production from fermentation. For mild disease, Lomotil is helpful in reducing the frequency of stools and pain. Care should be exercised, however, to avoid drugs such as Lomotil in cases of severe disease. By relieving pain, you may mask more serious problems. For mild disease, drugs such as Lomotil may contribute to the development of toxic megacolon. Azothioprine, one of the drugs used for cancer chemotherapy, is also effective in treating some cases of ulcerative colitis.

Crohn's Disease
(Granulomatous Ileitis, Ileocolitis, Regional Enteritis)

Crohn's disease is an inflammation of the bowel that primarily attacks the small intestine. Ulcerative colitis mainly involves the colon or large bowel. Some authorities believe Crohn's and ulcerative colitis to be two distinct conditions; others feel they are different expressions of the same disease process. The symptoms of the two conditions are similar and even the microscopic findings are often confusing. Both are provocative of arthritis.

In some instances, Crohn's disease may involve not only the small bowel, but also the colon and sometimes the duodenum as well. The inflammatory process may be intense, causing the thickening of all layers of the intestinal wall. This may be so severe as to cause the lumen—the opening through the intestine—to become blocked off, requiring surgery to correct. Characteristically, this inflammation hits some areas of the bowel and skips others. As in ulcerative colitis, the small bowel lining is rather devoid of nerve cells and severe inflammation and damage may be occurring without the individual being aware of it. As the lining is eroded, involvement of the deeper layers of the intestine is signaled by pain. Pain indicates the disease process is far advanced.

The symptoms of Crohn's disease are similar to those of other irritable bowel maladies: chronic diarrhea, pain, weight loss, fever, anorexia, and so forth. The condition may appear suddenly, presenting with an illness that can only be distinguished from appendicitis at surgery. More often, it presents as a chronic problem that comes and goes with severe colic and abdominal distension, constipation, and vomiting resulting from partial obstruction of the intestine. Persistence of these problems coupled with malabsorption of food (due to bowel inflammation, loss of digestive enzymes, and the loss of villi and bowel surface area) tends to weight loss and malnutrition.

Frequently, mild forms of this disease go unrecognized, and only those patients with severe cases come to medical attention. The more severe expressions of the disease are devastating. The erosive processes occasionally perforate the bowel wall and form passages or "sinuses" into other parts of the intestine, bladder, vagina, or even through the body wall out onto the skin. Obstruction of the bowel is most common. Many people with Crohn's have multiple surgeries to correct problems caused by the disease. This same erosive process may perforate the intestine and form abscesses within the abdominal cavity (in the pelvis or under the liver). It may also cause abscesses to form behind the peritoneum (the velamentous sac lining the abdominal cavity). Obstruction, fistulization, and abscess formation are common complications of Crohn's. Less common are intestinal bleeding, perforation, and small-bowel cancer. Anal fistulas (tunnels between the colon and the skin other than the anal opening) and anal fissures (ulcerated cracks in the anal opening) occur in about one-third of cases. The association between anal fistulas and Crohn's disease is such that the finding of an anal fistula is presumptive evidence of Crohn's disease. In many, the rectal pathology may be evident years before the bowel and systemic maladies become apparent.

Crohn's disease has many manifestations that are not expressed in the gastrointestinal system. Many of these wax and wane with the severity of the inflammatory process occurring in the bowel, usually in response to changes of diet. Commonly accompanying this disease are arthritis, aphthous stomatitis (canker sores of the mouth), erythema nodosum (painful reddened swellings of the skin that are scattered over the body), episcleritis (eye inflammation), pyoderma gangernosum (infection and death of portions of the skin), and recently noted psoriasis. These complications are twice as likely to occur if the colon is involved in addition to the small bowel.

Some extra-intestinal problems that have been found to accompany Crohn's disease do not remit and exacerbate in concert with the Crohn's activity; they are ankylosing spondylitis (a severe arthritis of the lower spine) and uveitis (inflammation of the iris). In children, Crohn's causes growth retardation, abdominal distension, anemia, chronic diarrhea, foul stools, poor resistance to diseases, abdominal pain, arthritis, and easily broken bones.

Crohn's and the other irritable bowel diseases cause excessive absorption of calcium, oxalate, urate, and bile acids. The first three contribute to kidney stone production (more on that later in this chapter), the latter to the formation of gallstones. Dr. Howard Spiro, professor of internal medicine at Yale University School of Medicine, suggests that the incidence of bowel cancer is increased in persons with Crohn's disease.

Surgery is frequently necessary to relieve bowel obstruction or to drain abscesses that form as a result of Crohn's. Often, diseased segments of the bowel must be surgically removed or bypassed. There is recurrence of the disease in about 95 percent of cases after surgery.

Antibiotics and cortisone are helpful in acute stages of the disease. The diagnosis is usually established by upper gastrointestinal and small-bowel series X rays.

At this time, it is unknown whether failure to digest the sugars eliminated in the ulcerative colitis/IBS diet is the cause or result of Crohn's disease. Among my own patients with Crohn's disease, all have responded to the elimination of fructose from their diets. One might expect such a result. Fructose is so readily fermented that fermentation begins early in the course of the food stream—in the small bowel. Wheat bran must undergo considerable enzymatic degradation before it is fermented and would tend to cause problems in the colon rather than in the small bowel. Hence, the kind of food with which one punishes the intestine may determine where the irritation will occur.

Celiac-Sprue

When the avoidance of lactose, fructose, wheat bran, mannitol, and sorbitol fails to stop one's irritable bowel symptoms, one should suspect gluten intolerance, known as celiac-sprue. (Other causes for failure may be infection, circulatory problems, diabetes, or possibly a tumor.)

For many years, an irritable bowel illness was noted in the tropics. It was given the name "tropical sprue." Later is was observed in nontropical countries where it was called "nontropical sprue" or "celiac disease." Vain searches were made to find an infectious agent responsible for this malady.

Celiac is one of the less common of the irritable bowel diseases. It is caused by an intolerance to gluten, the protein common to wheat, barley, oats, and rye. During World War II, food shortages in Europe afforded the clues leading to the discovery of the cause of this condition. It was noticed that a vegetable (mainly potato) diet brought relief to many of those who suffered chronic diarrhea at times when wheat and rye for bread became scarce. A Dutch doctor named Dicke found that eliminating wheat from the diet caused a marked improvement in many of these same individuals.

The definitive test for diagnosing celiac-sprue disease is a biopsy of the lining of the small bowel. To do this, a long tube with a capsulelike tip is swallowed. The capsule has a tiny open window and a spring-loaded windowsill knife. When X rays show the capsule to be in the small intestine, suction is applied to the external end of the tube, drawing a small piece of bowel lining in through the window of the capsule. At the same time, it releases the spring on the miniature knife. As the knife closes the window, it cuts off a small sample of tissue that has been drawn in through the opening. The capsule is then retrieved and the tissue sample removed for microscopic study.

Normally, with its myriad of tiny fingerlike projections called villi, this lining resembles the pile of a carpet. In celiac disease, the villi are lost or become short stumps, thereby greatly decreasing the absorptive surface area of the intestine. Also lost are the ends of the cells covering the villi. These cells normally support numerous hairlike projections called the brush border. The brush border is important because many of the digestive enzymes are produced on the bristles of the brush. When these are lost, many food substances fail to be digested. Undigested foodstuffs are fermented to produce lactic acid, alcohol, acetaldehyde, and other irritating chemicals that cause diarrhea. The failure to digest food, coupled with the rapid transit time of diarrhea, causes the sufferer to become malnourished. This malabsorption of nutrients in celiac disease closely resembles the starvation and malabsorption seen in ulcerative colitis, Crohn's disease, infections of the bowel, and other IBS disorders.

Celiac disease is thus related to the other irritable bowel diseases. Celiac sufferers share many of the problems of these other conditions. Fructose intolerance has not been recognized as being associated with gluten intolerance in celiac-sprue sufferers. However, I circulated a survey questionnaire among the participants of the Midwestern Celiac-Sprue Association convention held in October 1984, and one-third of the participants were aware that they were intolerant of lactose as well as gluten and had devised their diets accordingly. A nearly equal number had become aware that they did not tolerate foods high in fructose. Many in the survey were aware of "other food allergies." When questions relating specifically to tolerance of fructose and lactose sugars were presented, nearly one-third replied that sweet fruits, candy, ice cream, waffle syrup, and other fructose-rich foods caused exacerbations of their disease. No one had previously suggested to them that this sugar was the common element in the foods they were "allergic to." Eating these foods evoked symptoms indistinguishable from those of celiac-sprue. These respondents reported that they had discovered their intolerance to fructose-rich foods empirically, and that they now carefully avoided them in their diets. They did not know that these foods had the sugar fructose in common or that their symptoms were due to this sugar.

Other surprising findings were the association of arthritis (50 percent), kidney stones (20 percent), gallstones (50 percent), appendicitis (50 percent), and psoriasis. The occurrence rates of these associated complications were almost identical with those of the other irritable bowel diseases: ulcerative colitis, Crohn's, spastic colitis, and irritable bowel syndrome.

Many of the respondents to the colitis survey of the *Saturday Evening Post* volunteered the observation that wheat bran aggravated their bowel problems. It appears that many of those who are lactose and fructose intolerant are also bothered by wheat bran, the way celiac patients are bothered by fructose and lactose. These intolerances tend to interrelate, probably reflecting the loss of the brush border of the bowel lining. In the colitis survey, only three diagnosed celiac-sprue patients responded, but two of the three reported that they had been helped by avoiding fructose and lactose as well as wheat gluten.

The treatment of celiac disease is the rigorous avoidance of gluten-containing food. Sufferers are permitted meat and vegetable foods with rice and corn cereals. As mentioned above, one-third of these individuals must also avoid lactose and/or fructose. There are several organizations of celiac-sprue patients, and anyone with this problem would be greatly rewarded by joining one of them. The associations give out vital information on what you can eat with celiac-sprue, and where to buy special gluten-free foods. They also provide gluten-free recipes and conduct highly informative seminars. These associations are particularly helpful in giving patient information, as most doctors are not well informed about this rather rare malady.

Those with colitis, Crohn's disease, or any of the irritable bowel diseases should be aware of the possibility that they also have gluten intolerance. They should avoid the above-mentioned cereals if they prove to be irritating to their digestive systems. Persons with any of the irritable bowel diseases, including celiac-sprue, should avoid sorbitol and mannitol.

An Internet correspondent of mine posed a most provocative question: "Might there also be a mannitol intolerance?" To my knowledge, this question has not been asked before. In view of our knowledge of lactose intolerances, we should scrutinize each sugar for the possibility of failure to digest. Perhaps with celiac disease we have been looking at the wrong culprit. Perhaps the underlying problem is maltose intolerance rather than intolerance to gluten. This would more neatly explain celiac disease. Maltose is one of the steps in the breakdown of starch into glucose. Maltose consists of two glucose molecules joined. A failure to disjoin these molecules would cause the same kind of problem as failure to digest other sugars. Maltose is digested by the specific enzyme maltase. It stands to reason that there are people who are deficient in this enzyme. Deficiency of this enzyme would markedly impair the digestion of wheat, barley, oat, and rye starch.

It is probably significant that the protein gluten makes up a much smaller part of the grain, and starch a much greater portion. The starch must then go through the maltose-glucose conversion before it is absorbed by the intestine. The starch must be looked at with the same degree of suspicion we attach to gluten.

Radiation Colitis

Colitis often follows radiation therapy for cancer. Radiation injures, often permanently, the delicate bowel lining. As the mucosa is damaged, there is a reduction in the amount of digestive enzymes produced. As a result, many foods fail to digest and are passed into the lower digestive tract undigested. Fermentation follows and a vicious cycle of maldigestion, malabsorption, fermentation, and bowel irritation is established. Prominent among the foods that fail to digest are the sugars in the colitis diet. Most postradiation colitis victims will note improvement on the anticolitis diet. After allowing a few months for the bowel to repair itself, tolerance to these sugars may improve. Cancer chemotherapy may have the same effect as radiation injury to the intestine.

Drug-Induced Colitis

Many experience their first bouts of colitis following a course of antibiotics, especially after taking erythromycin or Cleocin. These drugs kill many normal bowel inhabitants but spare and seem to facilitate the growth of a bacterium called *Clostridium difficile*. This bacterium is a cousin to the tetanus and botulism organisms. It produces a powerful toxin that damages the bowel wall, producing a condition called pseudomembranous colitis, a severe and dangerous irritable bowel ailment. This results in the loss of the enzymes necessary to digest many foods. This irritable bowel condition is self-perpetuating; it interferes with the digestion not only of lactose and fructose but other foods that will ferment and cause further irritation. The anticolitis diet given in this book is the best means of correcting the problem. Avoiding the irritating sugars allows the bowel lining to heal. Reestablishing lactobacillus in the colon with yogurt or cottage cheese is prudent. In time, tolerance to these sugars improves though there may be some persistent intolerance.

Bowel lining injury by antibiotics (or other drugs) is one of the most common ways irritable bowel disease begins. Many individuals I have treated were unaware of any symptoms of food intolerance until they were given the antibiotics ampicillin or erythromycin by their doctors. When antibiotics cause colitis, it is time for immediate medical intervention. You probably will have to stop the antibiotics and take cortisone for one or two days. Then follow with the ulcerative colitis/IBS diet until normality returns.

Drug-induced colitis may follow many drugs including diuretics, those taken for high blood pressure, and anti-diabetes medications. Any of the antibiotics can irritate the bowel, causing colitis. Cancer chemotherapy can damage the intestine, resulting in colitis.

Secondary and Related Disorders

Pruritus Ani

One of the most agonizing symptoms of irritable bowel disease is pruritus, an irritation of the skin surrounding the anus. The condition is caused by a leakage of fecal liquid from the colon onto the skin surrounding the anus.

In irritable bowel disease, fermentation of fiber and sugars results in the production of lactic and acetic (plus other) acids, alcohol, acetaldehyde, and other irritating chemicals. When these chemicals come into contact with the skin, they inflame and destroy it. This results in a severe discomfort and itching.

An important point: the irritation on the outer skin is suggestive of similar serious irritation occurring internally. Remember, unlike the skin, the bowel lining has no pain nerves. Severe damage may be occurring internally with little in the way of symptoms to indicate anything is wrong.

Pruritus is not just an insignificant annoyance to be ignored. It is often the only warning of a more serious internal disease such as Crohn's disease or ulcerative colitis. In a report from Russia, one investigator found the occurrence of pruritus among victims of colon cancer to be near 100 percent. This does not say that pruritus causes bowel cancer, but that both share some common inciting factor or factors, and that pruritus may not safely be disregarded. Pruritus suggests that one is at risk for bowel cancer.

Pruritus may be the sole expression of digestive failure or, often, it is a symptom of more serious internal disease. When regarded as an independent entity, it is most often misdiagnosed as hemorrhoids and is treated with medications intended for that condition. When recognized as a symptom, it is a common element of any of the irritable bowel syndromes.

The immediate short-term treatment of pruritus is aimed at stopping the itching. Gentle washing of the anal area with soap and water gives immediate relief from pruritus. (Note that washing does not relieve thrombosed hemorrhoids.) Analgesic medications designed to treat hemorrhoids are to be avoided as they themselves are often irritating.

Wearing a small pad of three or four folded toilet tissue sheets tucked against the anus will absorb the caustic chemicals coming from the bowel. This is highly effective, but the emphasis should be on prevention rather than the treatment of this problem.

Topical corticosteroids relieve itching for a short while. These include:

- Vioform
- Mycolog
- Vytone
- Hytone
- Kenalog
- Cordran
- Over-the-counter preparations, such as Cortaid and Caldecort

Chronic usage of these medications rarely gives relief to those with pruritus. In chronic use, corticosteroids lose their effectiveness. Prolonging local treatment for pruritus will not cure the condition. Proper treatment must be directed at correcting the digestive problems causing the pruritus (i.e., avoiding the particular sugars responsible for lactic acid and acetaldehyde production).

My treatment consists of:

- Correcting the diet by eliminating offending sugars and fiber.
- Frequent cleansing with warm, soapy water.
- Corticosteroid creams for short-term management. (I prefer iodochlorohydroxyquin 3 percent, hydrocortisone 1 percent.) This has antibacterial and antifungal action as well as anti-inflammatory effects.
- Absorbent pads are very effective in keeping the area dry and keeping the acids and chemicals from the skin. Three or four sheets of toilet tissue folded into a pad one and a half inches wide and worn against the anus is highly effective. Change the pad two or three times a day. No belt or other device should be necessary to hold the pad in place.

When pruritus occurs, most people assume it is hemorrhoids and rush for the Preparation-H. Most doctors ascribe rectal itching to hemorrhoids, when in fact the symptoms of hemorrhoids are pain and swelling: small veins become inflated with blood from colonic spasm. Because these vessels have little muscle, they do not empty themselves and the blood stagnates and clots. There is pain, and a round, smooth, tender, marblelike nodule is felt at the side of the anus. *This* is hemorrhoids; itching is pruritus.

Diverticulosis and Diverticulitis

When fermentable materials reach the lower end of the bowel, the bacterial action of fermentation takes place, producing fairly large volumes of gas. Fermentation also produces alcohol, acetaldehyde, lactic acid, and other chemical byproducts of fermentation. These irritate the bowel and cause forceful contractions and cramping pains. These powerful contractions put the gas trapped in the colon under great pressure. This causes "blow-outs" in the thin, weak-walled portions of the colon. (See Figure 1.4.) The pressure of the gas causes hernias of the bowel wall at weak points, usually where blood vessels pierce the muscular layer of the intestine. Small sacs called diverticula form from these ruptures. Of themselves, they cause few symptoms. The underlying colitis causes gas, bloating, cramping, and other symptoms.

More than 50 percent of people over sixty years of age in the United States have some diverticula. This suggests that the irritable bowel problem is far more common than has been thought. It implies that more than 50 percent of senior citizens in the country fail to digest their food completely. The best treatment for this problem is to change the diet so less gas is produced. Relief can be

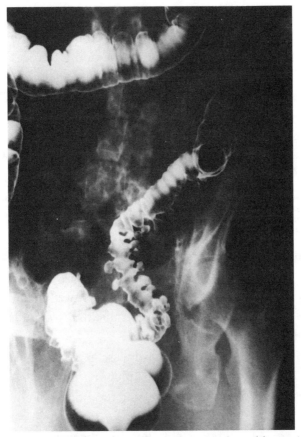

Figure 1.4: Diverticulitis. The numerous cherrylike projections from the barium-filled colon are the diverticula. These small out-pouchings are caused by the gas formed by fermentation of undigested food.

obtained by following the diet offered in this book and avoiding fructose, lactose, mannitol, sorbitol, wheat bran, and possibly maltose. For some, avoiding lettuce also helps considerably. Remember that the production of excessive wind or gas indicates a sugar intolerance. Diverticulosis indicates the presence of diverticula. Diverticulitis indicates infection of a diverticulum.

Diverticula are lined with bowel-lining mucosa. This layer has tiny mucous glands that lubricate the intestine. Should the opening from the bowel into the diverticular sac become plugged (as with a piece of nut, celery, or popcorn), the sac cannot drain. The trapped mucus soon teems with bacteria and the mucus becomes pus. An abscess has formed. Pressure builds within the sac and sharp pain is felt usually in the left side of the lower abdomen. This has all the signs of acute appendicitis, except it is on the left rather than the right side.

In the natural course of this disease, pressure builds in the diverticulum and blows the plug out into the bowel cavity. The diverticulum drains and the individual rapidly recovers.

When the plug does not blow out, the wall of the diverticulum breaks, spilling the pus and bacteria into the abdominal cavity, causing a sudden peritonitis. Peritonitis is life-threatening and calls for immediate surgical intervention. Peritonitis untreated is fatal.

Sometimes, infected diverticula erode through their own walls and through the walls of adjacent organs: the bladder, another loop of bowel, the uterus, or vagina. This allows a passage of stool material into the bladder or vagina. A fistula or tract is formed and one may have bowel movements through the vagina or bladder.

Antibiotics and pain medications are helpful during the acute illness of diverticulitis. It is important to be under the observation and care of a physician during this potentially disastrous illness.

Treating irritable bowel disease with proper dietary observance will do much to prevent diverticulosis and diverticulitis.

Kidney Stones

Stone formation in the urinary tract (renal lithiasis) has been recognized as a frequent complication of ulcerative colitis and Crohn's disease. This association prompted a 1985 survey of the Kidney Stone Formers Club, an organization sponsored by the *Saturday Evening Post*, to determine the converse situation. How frequently do irritable bowel diseases occur among stone formers? Analysis of 498 survey questionnaires suggested that at least 50 percent of kidney-stone formers have symptoms indicative of irritable bowel disease. This survey also suggested that many of these stone formers make their stones because of faulty digestion rather than faulty kidneys. Irritable bowel patients are all at risk for forming kidney stones, perhaps because the resulting acidic intestinal milieu allows too much calcium to be absorbed. The kidneys may not be able to handle the excess calcium. Other results of the survey are shown in Figure 1.5.

The high incidence of gastrointestinal symptoms in kidney-stone formers is striking. Intestinal gas production, frequent bouts of diarrhea, abdominal cramping, pains, and food intolerances point to a high incidence of irritable bowel disease among kidney-stone formers. Two hundred of the respondents indicated that they had excessive intestinal gas production, ninety had frequent bouts of diarrhea, and ninety-five reported abdominal cramping pains. The high frequency of these symptoms indicates that irritable bowel disease is extremely common among stone formers, but often has not been diagnosed as such. Irritable bowel disease is not only associated with kidney stones, it is often the cause of them. Question 10 indicates how many had been diagnosed as having lactose intolerance and question 11 shows that the number who get irritable bowel symptoms from ice cream (high in both lactose and fructose) is twice as great. Only eighteen were aware of fructose intolerance, but at least eighty either made gas or experienced diarrhea from orange juice, apples, or bananas. The recognized kidney-stone formation in Crohn's and ulcerative colitis, and the above frequent association of irritable bowel disease and renal lithiasis suggests a common mechanism for the formation of kidney stones that has not been fully appreciated.

Kidney Stone Formers Club Survey

Survey questions	*Yes answers*
1. Have you ever been diagnosed as having ulcerative colitis?	13
2. Do you have Crohn's disease?	8
3. Do you have spastic colitis?	39
4. Do you have celiac-sprue?	3
5. Do you have frequent bouts of diarrhea?	90
6. Do you have cramping abdominal pains?	95
7. Do you make excessive intestinal gas?	200
8. Do you have frequent bouts of constipation?	69
9. Do you have food intolerances?	105
10. Do you have lactose (milk sugar) intolerance?	45
11. Do you make intestinal gas after eating milk or ice cream?	93
12. Do you have pruritus (rectal itching) after eating milk or ice cream?	13
13. Do you have fructose (fruit sugar) intolerance?	18
14. Does orange juice cause gas or diarrhea?	69
15. Do bananas or apples cause gas or diarrhea?	80
16. Do you get pruritus after eating fruit?	15
17. Does candy cause gas or diarrhea?	31
18. Have you had hemorrhoids?	245
19. Have you had arthritis?	163
20. Have you had skin problems?	145
21. Have you had eczema?	59
22. Have you had psoriasis?	30
23. Have you had gallstones?	69

FIGURE 1.5: Kidney Stone Formers Club survey.

The failure to metabolize lactose has been acknowledged as a common cause of irritable bowel symptoms. Not previously recognized is a syndrome nearly identical to lactose intolerance but due to fructose intolerance. When these sugars are not digested and absorbed, they reach the lower digestive tract where their fermentation produces gases, alcohol, lactic acid, and acetaldehyde. Besides being highly irritating to the bowel mucosa, the acid lowers the pH of the fecal stream. As the bowel contents become more acidic, many calcium salts—such as calcium carbonate, the calcium salts of the bile acids, and calcium phosphate—that are insoluble in neutral or alkaline milieus become soluble. Lowering the pH by even small increments greatly increases the amount of calcium available for absorption into the bloodstream. The excess blood calcium is then presented to the kidneys for excretion. The increased calcium excretion load causes supersaturation of the urine and stone formation results. The kidneys, far from being culprits in stone formation, are the victims of excessive calcium absorption due to sugar fermentation in the gut. This appears to be a major mechanism for kidney-stone formation in IBS as well as in ulcerative colitis and Crohn's disease.

The survey also noted a high incidence of gallstones in kidney-stone formers. This appears to support the concept that irritable bowel disease provoked by lactose/fructose intolerance contributes to kidney-stone and gallstone development. When insoluble calcium salts of bile acid are subjected to acidification, both the calcium and the bile acid radicals become available for absorption. This allows continuous reabsorption and reexcretion of the bile acids causing supersaturation of the bile with these compounds. Gallstone formation is the consequence. Hence, the frequent association of gallstones and kidney stones.

The surprisingly high incidence of several conditions seemingly unrelated to kidney stones, such as hemorrhoids, arthritis, skin problems, and psoriasis perhaps reflects a common underlying digestive problem; these associations merit further research.

The implications of this survey suggest that for many stone formers, attention should be directed at correcting the problems arising from the gastrointestinal tract rather than trying to medically manipulate conditions in the kidneys. This means avoiding lactose and/or fructose, sorbitol, mannitol, and fiber. It is important to bear in mind that the kidneys cannot make calcium. They are, however, burdened with the task of excreting all the excess calcium the faulty gastrointestinal system absorbs. In the past we may have been looking too hard and in the wrong places to find the reasons for kidney-stone formation. We have made great efforts to find inhibiting substances that the "faulty kidneys" were not making. Lack of inhibitors does not account for hypercalcuria. By concentrating attention on the kidneys, we perhaps miss mildly symptomatic irritable bowel disease that causes excess calcium absorption and plays a major role in the development of many kidney stones.

Alzheimer's Disease

The irritable bowel diseases may predispose one to Alzheimer's disease. So far, there have been no detailed studies, but on theoretical grounds, these diseases may put one at a much greater risk for Alzheimer's. The acidification of the digestive system that occurs in irritable bowel disease increases the amounts of lead, mercury, cadmium, tin, zinc, and aluminum that will be absorbed. Several recent studies point incriminating fingers at aluminum as a possible cause of neurologic diseases such as Alzheimer's. Evidence for this comes from several fronts. Alzheimer's symptoms have been induced in cats, rabbits, monkeys, rats, and mice by giving them toxic amounts of aluminum. Memory, learning, and behavioral changes were observed in test animals. It was noted that younger animals were more resistant to aluminum intoxication than were older animals. The filaments of the brain cells of the aluminum-treated animals showed tangles that resemble those observed in the brain tissues of Alzheimer's victims.

Some individuals undergoing dialysis for kidney failure develop an Alzheimer's-like dementia. Ted L. Petit, Ph.D., of the Division of Life Sciences, University of Toronto,

Canada, reported in the *American Journal of Kidney Diseases:*

> Aluminum has been strongly implicated in human dialysis dementia. This syndrome is characterized by speech difficulties, motor abnormalities, personality changes, seizures, and progressive dementia terminating in convulsions and death. The syndrome is remarkably similar to the syndrome previously described in both experimental animals and non-diseased humans exposed to elevated levels of aluminum. A number of studies have shown that, particularly in the brain, aluminum is elevated in patients with dialysis dementia. A number of researchers have shown that dialysis dementia is associated with high aluminum content in the water used to make up the dialysate, and when deionized water is substituted, an elimination or reduction of dementia is observed.

According to another authority, Zavan S. Khachaturian, Ph.D., from the Physiology of Aging Branch, National Institute on Aging, of the National Institutes of Health, the Chamorros natives of Guam who ". . . have a remarkably high incidence of such degenerative disorders as amyotrophic lateral sclerosis and Parkinsons-dementia-lateral sclerosis complex, have high levels of aluminum in their brains." In Guam this condition accounts for 15 percent of all adult deaths. Nonnatives living in Guam for more than twenty years suffer the same fate.

Dr. Daniel Perl, of the Department of Pathology of the University of Vermont College of Medicine, used a highly sensitive scanning electron microscope in conjunction with spectrometry apparatus and identified abnormal accumulations of aluminum within the neurons (nerve cells) derived from patients with Alzheimer's disease.

Aluminum is the most abundant metallic element in the earth's crust, comprising about 8 percent. As it occurs in nature however, it is extremely insoluble and has been biologically unavailable until it was refined into its metallic state. Most of the aluminum absorption appears to come from refined metallic sources (for example, aluminum cooking vessels). More investigation into this relationship is ongoing and further developments will be forthcoming.

Skin Disorders

Several skin problems stem from irritable bowel disease. The most studied and best documented is the disease dermatitis herpetiformis, a blistering rash that accompanies celiac-sprue. Recent reports have also linked psoriasis and Crohn's disease.

Of the first 1,068 respondents to the Colitis Club survey, 169 reported that they had skin problems, and 81 reported psoriasis. Two hundred and four reported improvement after trying the Colits Club research diet—the diet given in this book—for a month.

Hemorrhoids

Almost all of our *Saturday Evening Post* survey respondents indicated they had experienced hemorrhoids. This would suggest that irritable bowel diseases cause hemorrhoids or that both have the same cause. There have been several theories explaining how hemorrhoids start. The most popular is one propounded by Dr. Denis Burkitt. Dr. Burkitt, observing African natives, came to the conclusion that his African patients did not get hemorrhoids because they ate a diet of coarse barley bread that was very fibrous. (He did not consider that the diet excluded sugars such as fructose and lactose.) Nevertheless, his theory that hemorrhoids are due to a lack of fiber in the diet has been accepted by the medical community, but there is not much evidence supporting it.

On numerous occasions, physicians delivering babies have observed hemorrhoids forming before their eyes. Pressure from the advancing infant and the mother's straining inflates the small veins about the anus. These veins are deficient in muscular coatings, and they are unable to empty themselves of blood. As a result, the stagnant blood caught in them clots and a hemorrhoid forms.

Many people have experienced the development of hemorrhoids during an attack of diarrhea. This poses a question: What do childbirth, diarrhea, and colitis have in common? One answer is that they all increase the pressure of the blood in the perianal veins. Straining does the same thing. In diarrhea and colitis, spasm of the lower bowel forces blood down the network of veins culminating at the anus. Hence most hemorrhoids are a result of spasm in the lower intestine. In diarrhea, this spasm often causes part of the rectal tissue to be forced out of the anus—turning the lower end of the bowel inside out, if you will. Usually this is very painful. The pain causes the anal muscles to contract and pinch the extruded bowel causing more pain. Some relief is accomplished by pushing the little mass of bowel back inside the anal valve.

Hemorrhoids, then, are small veins that have become inflated with blood that clots. They are very painful for about one week. They resolve themselves (or an adventurous physician will cut them open and express the clot—this sometimes lessens the pain). Often, the hemorrhoids rupture and bleed for several days, but this is not a reason to panic. Healing involves turning the hemorrhoid into a scar. It is then gone forever. There are, however, hundreds of little veins in the area that may inflate to make new hemorrhoids at a later day.

Pain medications such as acetaminophen, aspirin, and ibuprofen are helpful. An analgesic ointment such as Nuperacinal (no prescription required) is most beneficial.

Tucks—cloth patches soaked in witch hazel—also work. They burn like fire when you first tuck them against the hemorrhoid—after an hour they ease the pain by fatiguing the pain nerves. Keeping the area clean is very important. Swelling of the anus results in incomplete closure of the valve. Then bowel fluids leak onto the skin where they are very corrosive. They cause pain and itching and may progress to ulceration.

Contrary to the Preparation-H ads, itching is not a sign of hemorrhoids. Hemorrhoids are painful. Itching alone is pruritus, usually due to leakage of intestinal fluid onto the skin. (See section on pruritus on page 24.)

Rectal bleeding may come from hemorrhoids. It may also come from cancer in the lower bowel. You cannot tell which is causing the bleeding. Prudence demands bleeding be investigated by a physician.

Hemorrhoids are best avoided by following a diet that is not irritating to the intestines.

Gallstones

"Fair, fat, forty, female" were the four Fs medical students were once taught were the findings usually associated with gallstone disease. The implication was that somehow this constellation of symptoms caused gallstones to form. To the list I would propose adding other symptoms often arising from irritable bowel disease and associated with gallstones: kidney stones, pruritus, arthritis, and hemorrhoids. These symptoms are descriptive of irritable bowel disease as well as gallstones. Gallstones and irritable bowel disease are related. It is unlikely that gallstones cause irritable bowel problems; it is much more plausible that the opposite is true: irritable bowel diseases cause gallstones.

There are good reasons to suspect that irritable bowel disease is most often responsible for gallstones and flatulence in fair, overweight, fortyish females. In the past, doctors have often looked at each of these symptoms as an independent problem occurring alone or only coincidentally with the others. Here, I am attempting to show how some of these conditions interrelate and are traced to faulty digestion of sugars and/or wheat bran.

In the past, gallstones have been attributed to low-fiber diets, high-fat diets, white bread, and refined sugars. It is true that gallbladder disease is rare in underdeveloped countries where refined foods are not eaten. The high-fiber content of the diets in most of these countries may play a role, but evidence now points to the failure to assimilate the lactose and fructose in the diets of Western cultures as a more important cause.

While providing medical care to military dependents and retirees at Fort Benjamin Harrison in Indianapolis, I was amazed at how frequently these symptoms were found together in the same patients. Most of the Fort Harrison patients were middle-aged and had a wide variety of ailments, but approximately one out of every ten to twelve patients complained of bloating, chronic diarrhea, flatulence, and abdominal cramping pains. A high percentage of these patients had had their gallbladders removed; many of the same people had kidney-stone history, appendectomies, and hemorrhoids (these are almost universal in gallstone sufferers)—a whole gamut of intestinal complaints clustering in the same individuals.

Bile acid (cholic acid) is the body's principal means of disposing of cholesterol. The bile acids that are excreted from the liver and gallbladder into the intestine may be excessively reabsorbed. Normally some of the bile acid combines with calcium in the intestines to form an insoluble soap. When the food stream is neutral or alkaline, this insoluble combination passes out in the stool. In an acidic milieu, the calcium and bile acid dissociate and become soluble, and both are then absorbed. The calcium is carried to the kidneys where it may make stones. The bile acid is returned to the liver to be reexcreted in the bile. In irritable bowel disease, sugar fermentation results in the production of organic acids that acidify the food stream. This makes the calcium and bile acids available for reabsorption. Bile acids are excreted and reabsorbed repeatedly. This reabsorption and reexcretion of bile acid results in bile that is highly concentrated. In the gall bladder, water is removed from the bile. The thick, superconcentrated bile tends to separate, and cholesterol (bile acid) stones form in the gallbladder.

Calcium supplements, fiber, and an alkaline food stream facilitate the excretion of bile acids, thus reducing body cholesterol levels. However, fecal acidity interferes with cholesterol excretion. This has important implications for the health of the cardiovascular system. Irritable bowel disease reduces cholesterol excretion, resulting in an accumulation of cholesterol in the blood, and high cholesterol levels contribute to atherosclerosis. The conditions that lead to excessive bile reabsorption also cause excessive fatty-acid absorption; the excessive fat absorption makes obesity an inescapable fact of life for many unfortunate irritable bowel sufferers.

Constipation

Passive Constipation
As many people with irritable bowel disease complain of constipation as they do of diarrhea. Many complain of alternating between one and the other. Irritation of the bowel may cause both! Constipation is usually thought of as being due to a sluggish, lazy bowel that does not move things along. This form of constipation is a passive inertial condition in which waste just piles up. This is undoubtedly the cause of constipation in the elderly, and those with low thyroid levels often suffer this problem. Bowel stimulants or laxatives may be needed to correct

this condition. However, in irritable bowel disease, the irritated bowel tends to be hyperactive much of the time. It may move the food stream along too rapidly, causing loose stools.

Dynamic Constipation

In the normal action of the bowels, the muscles of the intestine contract and relax in a wavelike motion that moves the food stream through the intestine. With irritation of the bowel lining, the bowel may become spastic. With the bowel in spasm, all of the muscles are contracted at once and dynamic or spastic constipation results. The wave action cannot take place with all of the bowel muscles contracted. This form of constipation is often accompanied by cramping pains. Dynamic, or spastic, paralysis is as constipating as passive paralysis, but the treatment for the two is not the same. It is true that taking laxatives may work in both instances, but in the case of active paralysis, the best treatment is to relieve the irritation, and many laxatives tend to further irritate the bowel. In dynamic constipation, the cramps or spasms of the intestine may be very uncomfortable. By and by, segments of the colon fatigue and begin to relax and contract hyperactively, causing loose stools. Some irritable bowel victims never know constipation as they are continually plagued with diarrhea. Others with predominantly spastic colon may know only constipation. Many experience both.

The Gastrocolic Reflex

The gastrocolic reflex is a characteristic we share with most mammals. Feeding stimulates the bowel to defecation. If you tend to have the problem of constipation, you can often obey the call that will come just after morning or evening meals. Heeding nature's call may make laxatives or enemas unnecessary.

Restless Legs Syndrome

Several letters to the Colitis Club mentioned anxious legs. No one has linked restless legs and irritable bowel syndromes, but the frequent mention of the former by those with the latter at least raises the suspicion of an association. A few of the letters were published and a flood of "cures" was offered (everyone loves to play doctor). The letters prompted me to search the medical literature to see what the professors had to say about "restless legs syndrome," as it is referred to in medical writings.

Restless legs syndrome has been recognized for a long time. It was described by Thomas Willis in 1685. In the January 1986 issue of *AFP Journal*, Dr. Gary N. Fox summed up the state of our knowledge accumulated since Willis's time:

> Many pharmacologic agents have been reported to be effective in treating restless legs syndrome, although few

double-blind studies of drug therapy have been recorded. No surgical or physical modalities have proved consistently beneficial.

Recognized as a common cause of insomnia, restless legs syndrome most often acts up when the sufferer is retiring to bed. It causes hyperesthesia—a greatly amplified sensation of touch. The legs cannot tolerate the touching of one by the other, the touching of bedclothes, or being touched by another person. (Paradoxically, slight touches provoke the most unpleasant sensation.) There is also an intolerance to heat. Even in very cold environs, sufferers will tend to sleep with the feet uncovered. Complete temporary relief comes from walking about—but one cannot get any sleep that way. Restless legs also annoy when sufferers are sitting still in meetings, movies, church, classes, and while traveling in planes, autos, and trains. Several doctors reporting in the *Archives of Internal Medicine* tried to find some common elements that could link twenty-seven cases to some related cause and noted that the malady tended to be hereditary. Ten of the cases also had headaches and insomnia, seven had back pains, and three had irritable colon problems. The syndrome plagued my mother, as well as her brother and two sisters. I and those relatives all share fructose intolerance–induced irritable bowel disease as well as restless legs syndrome.

I noticed that attacks came while sitting in movie houses, almost invariably near the end of the movie. My legs would want to jump up and climb the screen. Sitting in school or church only rarely provoked an attack. I was led to conclude that the candy bar I ate at the beginning of the show was the provoking element. Following this lead, I noted that each time I had a large amount of sugar late in the day, the evening was marked with the agony of crawly legs. Other members of my family found they, too, could provoke the condition by eating sugar. These family members also shared irritable bowel syndrome.

Several respondents to the Colitis Club survey commented on their questionnaires that since they had been on the colitis diet and avoided lactose, fructose, sorbitol, and mannitol, their restless legs have not bothered them. Perhaps we have discovered one cause of restless legs syndrome. Speaking for myself, I do not suffer from restless legs when I follow the diet.

Hyperinsulinemia

Many individuals produce too little insulin. Because of this, they have great difficulty in metabolizing glucose for energy. We call this condition diabetes. Others have the opposite situation, a condition that has received little attention: the production of too much insulin. Usually this happens in response to the ingestion of large amounts of sugar. The large sugar dose appears as a huge meal to the system, and in anticipation a large amount of insulin is released. The insulin rapidly causes the blood sugar levels to drop, sometimes causing fainting or collapse. The action of the insulin lasts several hours. The excess insulin reduces the blood sugar levels to undesirable values. Hyperinsulinemia has been described as a leading predictor of myocardial infarctions.

Sugar taken late in the day is apt to cause excess insulin to be produced that, in turn, causes low blood sugar. Nerves are very sensitive to shortages of oxygen or glucose. When the blood sugar falls, the nerves of the feet and legs complain with the sensation described by neuritis victims. Most restless legs occur in those who produce too much insulin.

Restless legs can be prevented by avoiding sugar boluses such as candy, cake, and ice cream late in the day. Eating generous amounts of starch late in the day also helps avoid low blood sugar by its slow conversion to sugar over several hours. Sugar gives immediate relief, but may spark the release of more insulin. It is advisable to include starch with the sugar to maintain adequate blood sugar levels over several hours while you sleep.

Hypoglycemia

Whether or not hypoglycemia is related to irritable bowel disease is unknown, but a number of colitis correspondents have written that they suffered from low blood sugar. Many complained that their doctors told them, "There is no such thing." But low blood sugar does occur, paradoxically, after eating large amounts of sugar. Much of the information circulated about hypoglycemia is not factual, and current treatment tends to aggravate the condition rather than help it. Often the treatment is worse than the ailment.

Sugar, specifically glucose, is the "gasoline" the body was designed to run on. When blood sugar gets too low, you feel like you are out of gas, weak, and tired. Common activities require great effort. Other symptoms may follow such as malaise, nausea, severe headache, sweating, irritability, and depression.

Oddly, the common form of hypoglycemia is related to excess sugar ingestion. In the past, our ancestors' diet was devoid of concentrated sugars, and so we have not developed the facility to handle sudden large surges of sugar. It has been only in the past fifty years that sugar in large amounts has been available to the general population. Overingestion of sugar is common in our present diets, but in the past, sugar had been a great luxury in the form of small amounts of honey.

Fructose presents a special problem. It easily provokes insulin production. Because it is poorly absorbed by many, it does not get into the blood to utilize the insulin it has stimulated, and hyperinsulinism results.

When a person ingests a large amount of table sugar, it is rapidly absorbed into the blood. Absorption begins in the mouth and continues in the stomach (other foods are not absorbed until they get into the small intestine). This rapid absorption of sugar abruptly raises the glucose level. When the blood sugar rises, the body supposes it to be an enormous meal and calls for a correspondingly

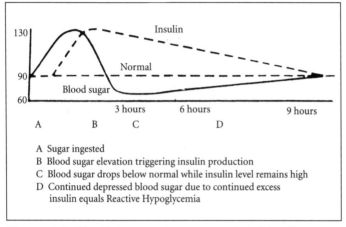

Figure 1.6: Blood sugar response to starch and insulin.

large amount of insulin to deal with it. In some persons, much more insulin is released than is actually needed for the amount of sugar present. The blood sugar elevation lasts for about an hour, after which the excess insulin begins to rapidly decrease the blood sugar. Suddenly, the level falls below normal and hypoglycemia is present. The activity of the insulin lasts from two to twelve hours. The excess insulin may maintain the blood sugar below normal for several hours. (See Figure 1.6.)

To prevent the blood sugar from falling too low, the body releases adrenaline that acts to increase blood sugar. Conflicting forces come into play. The insulin is trying to reduce the blood sugar further, and the adrenaline trying to raise it. It is like trying to drive your car with one foot on the accelerator and the other on the brake.

Most of the symptoms experienced in hypoglycemia are due to the effects of the adrenaline rather than the low blood sugar: sweating, trembling, heart palpitation, giddiness, nervousness, and anxiety. Severe or dangerous hypoglycemia is rare. Occasionally, hypoglycemia is of severe enough degree to cause unconsciousness and possibly seizures. If blood sugar levels are only slightly decreased, symptoms are usually not noticed. As lower levels are reached, symptoms begin to appear. Normally blood sugar ranges from 70 to 100 milligrams per 100 cc of blood. Most people maintain a level of about 90 milligrams most of the time. As levels fall to the 60 milligrams per 100 cc level, drowsiness, laziness, and weakness are likely to be noticed. As a lower level of 50 milligrams is reached, more pronounced symptoms appear. Here is where adrenaline begins to be produced to prop up the falling sugar and protect vital structures such as the brain from energy deprivation; sweating is noted, the heart beats faster and pounds. Headache is apt to occur and confusion develops as the brain gets insufficient fuel.

As the blood sugar drops further, personality changes occur. The person may become irrational, belligerent, and combative; speech is garbled; and as the sugar level drops further, coma ensues and seizures are likely because the brain now has too little sugar for its energy requirements. If the sugar drops more, brain cell damage or death is likely since glucose is the only fuel brain cells can use for energy. Depriving the brain of either oxygen or glucose for only a few minutes injures or destroys it. Such extremely low blood sugar levels usually occur with accidental insulin overdosage for diabetes.

To prevent these periods of low blood sugar from happening, one must avoid large boluses of sugar that overstimulate insulin release. A breakfast of waffles or pancakes and syrup is the surest way to overload with sugar. Eating candy or drinking soda pop in place of a meal will often result in hypoglycemia. Ice cream eaten alone produces a sharp rise in blood sugar that may be followed by a sharp fall.

Eating a breakfast that is mainly starch, such as cereal, is the best way to avoid low blood sugar. The process of digesting starch involves its conversion into glucose in the intestine, then its absorption into the blood. Starch also stimulates insulin production but only after it has been partially changed into sugar. The process of changing the starch into sugar avoids the rapid absorption of glucose; rather, the glucose is fed into the blood over a longer period of time and huge releases of insulin do not occur. The treatment of hypoglycemia consists of eating starches and avoiding large quantities of sugar.

Hypoglycemia is the opposite condition to diabetes. In diabetes, there is decreased insulin and sugar accumulates in the blood. The main part of the treatment is to reduce the amount of sugar eaten (this includes sugar that will come from converted starch). Here a low-carbohydrate, high-protein diet may be appropriate. You would not treat the diabetic who has too much sugar by giving him more sugar; neither would you treat the hypoglycemic who has too little sugar by giving him less sugar. But this is exactly what is most often recommended for hypoglycemia: a low-carbohydrate, high-protein diet. What is needed is a high-starch diet, more like our ancestors ate eons ago, the diet the human body was designed for. Figure 1.6 shows the blood sugar response to starch and insulin: a slow release of sugar into the blood.

Cancer

Colon Cancer
Irritable bowel disease greatly predisposes one to cancer of the colon. Each year 2½ percent of those with ulcerative colitis develop cancer. That may not sound like many, but it amounts to 25 percent each ten years and 50 percent every twenty years! This alone makes it imperative to treat bowel conditions in the very best manner and to initiate a surveillance plan to detect cancer as early as possible. Following the dietary guidelines of this book will reduce the inflammation of the bowel lining, thereby reducing its susceptibility to cancer.

There are a number of theories as to why bowel cancer develops. One is that bile acids irritate the intestinal wall when there is slow transit time of the food stream. Another is the lack of fiber in the diet. Yet another is the invasion of the bowel lining by any one of a number of cancer-causing viruses that abound in the foods we eat from animal sources. (Vegetarians have been recognized to have very low cancer rates for five decades.) Irritation by those elements responsible for irritable bowel syndrome allows these carcinogenic viruses to colonize and start a tumor. These viruses come from animal foods that have not been sufficiently cooked to destroy all of the germs that are present. Virtually all the cancers occurring in the animal kingdom are traced to these viruses. Many human tumors have been traced to viruses as well.

Many people insist on eating meat that has not been thoroughly cooked. What they fail to realize (or no one ever told them) is that between 20 and 30 percent of all cattle are infected with bovine leukemia virus. This virus is closely related to the AIDS agent. It causes cancer in the cattle. Eating rare meat often involves the consumption of this virus in an infective state. Since no one has ever found antibodies to bovine leukemia virus, it has been assumed harmless and no threat to humans. (It grows well in human cell cultures.) If this virus invades a human cell and transforms it into a cancer cell, the body would produce no antibodies. Our beneficent government has passed laws giving them control of all substances that appear to cause cancer in rats and mice—they completely ignore the agents causing cancer in the animals from which we eat meat, milk, and eggs! Twenty-five percent of all the dairy cows in this country are infected with bovine leukemia virus. These animals shed it in their milk. Since nearly one-third of the cows harbor this agent, all of the commercial milk is contaminated. At least one study has suggested that pasteurization does not eradicate the virus from commercial milk.

Other sources of cancer-causing viruses are eggs and chickens. Since no one eats rare chicken, consumption of cooked chicken poses little or no danger. The eating of raw eggs (as in eggnog or some Caesar salads) is probably dangerous. Also dangerous, is the eating of soft or over-easy eggs. These eggs are not heated sufficiently to kill the fowl leukosis and Marek's viruses that cause cancer in the chickens. Laying hens are usually butchered when they become two years old, not because they have stopped laying (they are in the prime of their egg-laying careers) but because they begin dying of cancer at that age. I recall personally butchering hens with three different kinds of cancer. No one has found antibodies to fowl leukosis virus in humans—so the virus has come to be regarded as harmless. But again suppose one fowl leukosis virus invades one human cell and starts a cancer—no antibodies would be formed by the body.

To avoid bowel cancer, and most other common cancers, it is prudent to maintain a healthy bowel lining and cook meat, eggs, and milk thoroughly. For more evidence supporting this concept, the reader may refer to my book on the Navaho Indians, *Their Secrets: Why Navaho Indians Never Get Cancer*.

Recent studies have reported that prostaglandin inhibitors, the family of pain-relieving drugs to which aspirin, ibuprofen, and naproxin belong, get rid of intestinal polyps, the precursors to bowel cancer. Cardiologists recommend an aspirin per day to prevent heart attacks and strokes. It would be prudent for those with irritable bowel disease to do likewise to eliminate bowel polyps.

Cancer Surveillance

Checking the stool for occult blood is important to detect cancers of the bowel as early as possible. This is doubly important for those with irritable bowel disease. If there is a common denominator among those who get bowel cancer, it is irritable bowel disease.

Cancers are disorganized tissues that invade blood vessels and cause them to leak. The simplest means of detecting bowel cancers is to test the stool for traces of blood. The test is not infallible, but it is still very good. There are several good home tests for this purpose, such as Hemoccult, Fleet Detectatest, and CS-T Colo Screen Self Test to name a few. Hemoccult and Detectatest require the smearing of a small quantity of stool on a paper and applying a drop of peroxide; the presence of blood is indicated by a purple color. CS-T Colo Screen requires only the floating of a special tissue on the water in the commode to detect blood. The merits of these tests can be debated. It is more important to do any of them than to be concerned over which is best. It is important to stop taking vitamin C three days before doing these tests, as vitamin C will cause a false negative test. Some foods such as turnips and radishes may also interfere.

Any visible blood in the stool should be investigated. The American Cancer Society advises an inspection of the inside of the bowel by proctoscopy annually. In view of their increased risk, this is especially good advice for victims of irritable bowel disease. There are several possible causes of blood in the stool other than cancer. Hemorrhoids often rupture and leave bright red blood on the toilet tissue. Large hard stools may tear the lining of the rectum, again leaving stains on the tissue. Bleeding is a common occurrence with more severe ulcerative colitis. Diverticulosis often causes bleeding that at times may be massive. The stalks of polyps, molelike growths from the bowel wall, may tear and cause bleeding. Polyps are important as it is generally believed that cancer most often begins on the ends of these growths. A positive test is not reason for despair, but it is the signal to get help as soon as possible.

Examinations of the Colon

There are two means of examining the interior of the bowel: barium enema X rays and direct inspection with a proctoscope or colonoscope. The barium enema involves the flowing of liquid barium sulfate into the colon and recording its shadows on X-ray film. Generally, the flow of the barium is observed by the radiologist with a fluoroscopic plate or an image intensifier. X-ray plates are exposed periodically. The procedure is usually followed by air contrast studies. After the colon is filled with barium and the X-ray plates are exposed, the barium is evacuated from the bowel. A thin layer of barium adheres to the bowel wall. The colon is then inflated with air. Many details obscured by the barium enema then become apparent.

The colonoscopic examination is usually made with a flexible telescope inserted into the colon. Examinations are made of the lining at various distances into the colon. This procedure is particularly helpful in the lower colon where spine and pelvis shadows may obscure the X-ray details of the bowel. These examinations are complementary—both are important.

Bowel Infections and Infestations

Chronic infections of the digestive system may closely mimic irritable bowel syndrome. Most bacterial and viral infections produce symptoms of pain, diarrhea, weakness, and fever that are very much like acute exacerbations of ulcerative colitis or Crohn's disease. Irritable bowel diseases caused by bacterial infections tend to be short-lived. Most often, they begin rather suddenly, causing a severe illness that remits in one to seven days. Even cholera and typhoid are self-limited in healthy individuals.

Infections of the bowel by protozoans (one-celled animal parasites) tend to be chronic, often lasting for years. These germs of the amoeba family cause symptoms similar to those of irritable bowel disease caused by sugar intolerance. Protozoans usually come from eating or drinking contaminated food or water. Because the symptoms are similar, it is prudent for those with irritable bowel disease to have stool studies for parasites, and an eosinophile blood count. (This family of white blood cells increases in response to parasitic infestations.) These microbes are also communicated between homosexual men. Once rare in this country, these pathogens have become fairly common due to sexual activity between infected persons.

Giardia lamblia is perhaps the most common protozoan parasite in this country. It is most often contracted by hunters and campers who drink water from creeks without boiling it. The tiny animal produces an illness that is clinically similar to irritable bowel syndrome. It is sometimes difficult to diagnose, requiring small bowel biopsy (see discussion on celiac-sprue on page 17).

The other important protozoans, *Endamoeba histolytica*, *Endamoeba coli*, and *Balantidium coli* are responsible for amebic dysentery. These are diagnosed by examination of the stool and are suspected when the eosinophil count is elevated. The ulcerative colitis/IBS diet will help these conditions but will not eliminate them. Specific antibiotics are effective; usually Flagyl is prescribed.

Hiatus Hernia

A hiatus hernia occurs when the esophageal opening in the diaphragm allows part of the stomach to escape from the abdomen into the chest cavity (see Figures 1.7A and B). This may come about as a result of a congenitally enlarged esophageal opening in the diaphragm. Others develop this hernia from a severe blow to the abdomen, as in an auto accident or an explosion.

Irritable bowel disease is also a cause of hiatus hernia. In irritable bowel disease, the gaseous inflation of the bowel compromises the available space in the abdomen. This causes a constant upward pressure on the stomach—forcing part of the organ into the chest. Often, the person suffering this condition is obese, and the fat stores in the abdomen further encroach on the available space in the abdomen—adding to the upward pressure on the stomach.

Aging also plays a role, as weakness of the diaphragm muscle allows the hiatus, or esophageal opening to relax and enlarge. This permits some of the stomach to be pressed into the chest space between the lungs and behind the heart.

Weight reduction and antigas measures such as the colitis diet should be tried before surgery is contemplated. For those with severe symptoms, surgery may be curative, but the cure rate for the surgical treatment is around a dismal 50 percent.

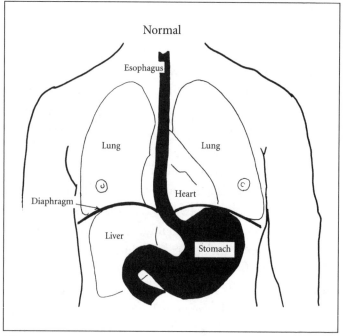

Figure 1.7a: Normal stomach position.

Coxa Fugax

Coxa fugax literally means pain in the coccyx region. This is an intense pain resulting from a spasm of the muscles that surround the bottom of the colon. Irritable bowel is probably the cause. It is more commonly associated with diarrhea. The pain lasts about an hour then goes away as mysteriously as it comes, most commonly at night. The tendency to get coxa fugax is probably inherited.

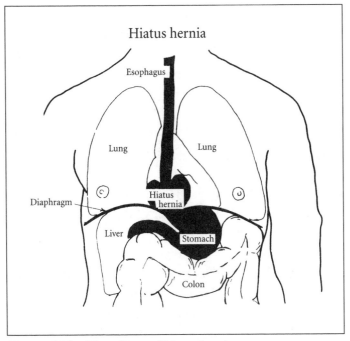

Figure 1.7b: The effects of hiatus hernia.

Normally, peristaltic waves, the periodic contractions and relaxations of the bowel, propel food in one direction from top to bottom, or mouth to rectum. Under some circumstances, such as obstruction, the peristaltic waves move in the reverse direction. (People with bowel obstruction can actually have fecal vomiting.) Fugax may be the result of a normal forward moving peristaltic wave colliding with a reverse wave that starts from the end of an irritated colon. Although not dangerous, fugax is painful and distressing.

Treatments include pain medications such as Tylenol, aspirin, and ibuprofen. It may help to sit on a commode or in a tub of hot water. Surgical procedures have been described, but would appear unwise as the attacks usually last but an hour.

Leaky Gut

One of the more serious effects of irritated bowel is the breach of the protective barrier of the bowel lining. Inflammation and erosion of the mucosal layer of the intestine allows bacteria and noxious chemicals to enter the absorptive channels. Once in these channels, the hostile foreign matter is "mainlined" up the portal vein into the liver. The liver is then faced with detoxifying noxious chemicals and arresting bacteria that have escaped from the intestinal contents. Serious damage is done to the liver, which may become completely destroyed and replaced with scar tissue—cirrhosis.

How Do You Know If You Have a Problem?

Intestinal Gasses

The production of intestinal gas, or flatus, is the sure sign that undigested sugars or fiber are being fermented. The production of large volumes of flatus is a pretty sure sign of trouble. Whenever fermentation occurs, it produces alcohol, some of which oxidizes into acetaldehyde, a close relative of formaldehyde (embalming fluid). Acetaldehyde is extremely irritating; its medical use is for killing warts. Also produced is an array of gasses: hydrogen, methane, carbon dioxide, ammonia, and hydrogen sulfide.

There are only a few sources of intestinal gasses. One source is swallowed air. Some swallow air unconsciously while eating or chewing gum. Others do it to induce belching for temporary relief of stomach discomfort. Much of the swallowed air is absorbed into the blood and escapes through the lungs. Some gas is formed as carbonates reach the stomach. Here the hydrochloric acid changes carbonates into carbon dioxide gas. Large volumes of carbon dioxide will cause burping. Smaller amounts will be absorbed into the blood and carried to the lungs for excretion.

Lower intestinal gas is formed by fermentation of foodstuffs in the bowel. The particular gasses formed depend on which bacteria are acting on the food substrates that reach the bowel. Social decorum mandates that this gas is not to be discharged in the presence of others. As we retain intestinal gas, particularly in an irritated bowel, very high pressures build. These gasses are important for two reasons: they are unpleasant, and the gas confined in the irritated cramping bowel causes the small herniations of diverticulosis in the walls of the colon. Fermentation by a host of different bacterial varieties is akin to burning. It produces a multitude of chemical wastes including lactic and acetic acids in addition to the gasses, alcohol, and acetaldehyde. It also makes hundreds of other chemicals—a few are beneficial, many are harmless, some are very harmful and circulate to affect joints, eyes, lungs, liver, and skin. Hence if you are making significant intestinal gas, you are also making chemicals injurious to your intestine and other organs.

Carbon Dioxide

The intestinal gas formed in greatest quantity is carbon dioxide. It is formed when fats, proteins, or carbohydrates are fermented. This gas readily dissolves in the blood and is carried to the lungs where it is excreted. Carbon dioxide is a harmless waste produced by burning foods. It is compressed into water to make carbonated water as in soda pop.

Ammonia and Hydrogen Sulfide

When there is a failure of the intestine to digest and absorb lactose or fructose, the resulting irritation to the intestine impairs protein digestion and absorption. The unabsorbed protein is then available for bacterial fermentation.

Fermentation of protein releases ammonia. Chemically, the amino acids that make up proteins are short carbohydrate chains similar to sugars with an ammonia (nitrogen) group attached. (Ammonia is the compound resulting when one nitrogen and three hydrogen atoms combine.) Burning amino acids releases the ammonia radical; the remaining carbohydrate portion is then burned to water and carbon dioxide. Much of the ammonia produced by fermentation is absorbed into the blood where it is converted to urea. The urea is then excreted via the kidneys. Some of the ammonia may be passed as flatus (the ammonia contributing to the unpleasant odor). Some of the amino acids in protein also contain sulfur. When sulfur containing amino acids is fermented, hydrogen sulfide or "rotten egg" gas is produced. This gas imparts a most disgusting odor to the flatus.

Methane and Hydrogen

Methane and hydrogen complete the list of important gasses produced by colonic fermentation. These gasses are insoluble in water or blood and only small amounts of them diffuse into the blood and are excreted through the lungs. Most pass as flatus. These gasses are related to fuel natural gas and are highly combustible. A few patients have been killed or seriously injured in the course of bowel examinations when electro-cautery was used through a colonoscope to destroy polyps. The spark ignites a collection of methane/hydrogen gas that explodes.

The Reaction Delay

The identification of foods that cause irritable bowel diseases is made difficult by the time lapse between eating a food, and the appearance of gas or symptoms. The delay may range from ten to twenty-four hours. It is hard to relate the milk or ice cream eaten yesterday with the gas and diarrhea experienced today, but this is the usual picture. It takes the unabsorbed sugars several hours to reach the lower digestive tract where the fermentation occurs. Then the fermentation takes place over several hours.

When fructose, lactose, or wheat gluten fail to be digested and absorbed, they become fermented by the bacteria in the bowel. This results in a whole chain of chemical events, some with damaging consequences. When examining a few of these chemical reactions from a chemist's point of view, the most striking consequence is the production of large volumes of gas. The fermentation of one-quarter pound of one of these sugars produces about twenty quarts of gas (it seems much more). The gas distends the abdomen and causes the bloating and flatulence of irritable bowel disease.

Chapter 2

The Causes of IBS Disorders

Intestinal Diabetes

Flooding the lower intestinal tract with fructose and lactose is in some ways similar to diabetes. Instead of excessive glucose accumulating in the blood, excessive amounts of these sugars pool in the bowel. With this accumulation, bacterial fermentation occurs. (Even though the individual may lack the enzymes necessary to digest these sugars, some of the myriad of bacterial inhabitants of the bowel are able to metabolize them into gas, alcohol, acetaldehyde, lactic and acetic acids.) The concept of "diabetes of the bowel" is helpful in dietary planning to prevent indigestible sugar and fiber overload (see Figure 2.1).

The lactic acid, alcohol, and acetaldehyde produced by the fermentation irritate the bowel resulting in diarrhea, mucus production, bleeding, and sloughing of the lining. In the irritable bowel diseases, a vicious cycle develops.

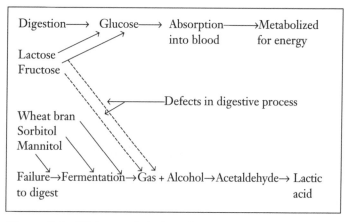

Figure 2.1: Diabetes of the bowel.

Lactic acid, alcohol, and acetaldehyde burn the bowel lining, causing the enzyme-producing lining to be sloughed out. This further impairs lactose and fructose digestion, which in turn allows more fermentation to make more lactic acid and acetaldehyde.

The use of the diet given in chapter 4 entails a little detective work. You may be intolerant of lactose and tolerant of fructose. In this situation you may have all the fruit you want. Or, you may be tolerant of lactose but intolerant of fructose. In this case, you may have milk but must avoid orange juice, apples, grapes, bananas, other sweet fruit, and corn sweetener. Personally, I can tolerate lactose in any quantity, but develop symptoms after small amounts of fructose (one apple or banana, or one Twinkie). If you have active irritable bowel disease, you are probably intolerant of both sugars. In this case you must avoid milk and fruit sugars.

For individuals having active disease, gas, diarrhea, cramps, pruritus, and other symptoms, I recommend avoidance of all items listed on the diet. The intestine irritated by one sugar is less tolerant of other sugars. Once bowel injury has taken place and has resulted in malabsorptive disease, the array of symptoms looks pretty much the same irrespective of which offending agent started it. The injured bowel fails to digest a number of food stuffs that pass into the lower tract to be fermented by bacteria. Fructose intolerance may initially injure the bowel lining, making it fail to digest other foods such as lactose or wheat bran. The symptoms are identical, irrespective of the offending agent or agents.

In the hospital study, it was noted that many people have a partial intolerance to these sugars. This suggests a threshold phenomenon. Some tolerate small amounts of these sugars with no apparent ill effects. When larger amounts are ingested, gas, diarrhea, cramping, and rectal irritation ensue. No fructose or lactose is to be permitted during active irritable bowel disease. Once the bowel lining has become irritated, even small amounts of these sugars exacerbate the symptoms.

Several individuals traced the onset of their disease to an episode of antibiotic treatment. When an antibiotic causes the loss of or injury to the intestinal lining, most people lose the ability to digest a number of food substances including fruit and milk sugars. Bowel lining injury by antibiotics (or other drugs), is one of the most common ways irritable bowel disease begins. The bowel injury unmasks a deficiency in digestive enzyme production. Many individuals I have treated were unaware of any symptoms of food intolerance until they were given antibiotics such as ampicillin or erythromycin by their doctors. Many drugs may injure the bowel lining, initiating malabsorption and its associated problems. The injury may then be self-perpetuating. The initial injury may cause or intensify fructose and lactose malabsorption. Malabsorption leads to more fermentation, which in turn irritates the bowel more, causing more malabsorption.

In the intestine, most carbohydrates are converted to glucose before they are absorbed. Starch is not absorbed into the blood as starch; it is first converted to glucose.

(This is why diabetics must limit bread and potatoes as well as sugar.) Lactose is not absorbed as lactose; it first has to be converted to glucose, which is actively absorbed. The same is true of fructose. Failure to make these conversions leads to the problems of irritable bowel disease described in this book. Carbohydrates that are not converted to glucose are not absorbed. They remain in the intestine, becoming substrate for fermentation. Fiber such as wheat bran is indigestible by humans. We cannot convert it to glucose. Yeasts and some of the microorganisms in the intestine can break down fiber; it then becomes substrate for fermentation.

Enzyme Deficiency

The lack of digestive enzymes for specific food elements is the basis for most irritable bowel diseases. Lack of enzymatic competence for changing lactose or fructose to glucose underlies most irritable bowel diseases. Insufficiency of other enzymes also allows undigested food to ferment in the intestine.

Enzymatic deficiency may be present for specific food elements, often such deficiencies are multiple. Deficiency of one enzyme may result in multiple deficiencies, as the products of fermentation from undigested food may injure the bowel lining so it produces less of other enzymes. Failure to digest (and absorb) multiple foodstuffs results in malnutrition. (Note: taking vitamins and minerals will not correct protein or carbohydrate deficiencies.)

The end result of the irritable bowel diseases is malabsorption and malnutrition. The loss of the epithelial brush border that lines the small intestine with its enzyme production causes failure to digest foods. Foods are not broken down and consequently not absorbed. The undigested, unabsorbed foodstuffs pass into the lower digestive tract where they ferment. This produces toxic substances that irritate the bowel wall. The toxic products of fermentation pass into the blood and cause harm in the liver, joints, skin, eyes, and other organs. Severe diarrhea with cramps and mucus production follows with weight loss, anemia, and malnutrition.

Artificial Enzyme Replacement

The primary strategy, given in chapter 4, is the avoidance of the foods that most commonly fail digestion. Enzyme replacement therapy is a second option for some of those with malnutrition caused by enzymatic insufficiency. One ploy that has helped some irritable bowel sufferers is to replace the lost enzymes with plant or animal enzyme preparations. This is particularly useful in situations where a large portion of the intestine has been removed or has been injured by radiation treatments.

One common enzyme supplement is lactose replacement (Lactaid or Lactrase) to aid in the digestive process of turning lactose into glucose. (There is no comparable enzyme product available to convert fructose to glucose.) The number of enzyme replacements is limited, and they tend to be expensive. Most come as tablets or powders to be taken with meals or mixed in the food. The enzyme supplements are remarkably safe.

Supplements provided by the drug companies include:

- Kanulase
- Cotazyme
- Kuzyme
- Arcolose
- Festal
- Viokase

Others are available over the counter through health food stores (where they are usually called "essential enzymes"). These products are mixtures of enzymes derived from the pancreases of animals or from pineapple. They are good sources of proteolytic (protein-digesting) and amylase (starch-reducing) enzymes. They are not very good at the conversion of fructose to glucose. Because the enzymes are made of protein, most oral supplements are digested high in the digestive tract and do not get down to the lower intestine where they are needed. Thus oral agents may prove disappointing. In view of their great safety, however, they should be given a try.

A surprising number of my patients with malabsorption get significant benefit from the enzyme in meat tenderizer. They mix half a teaspoon of Adolph's Meat Tenderizer with their food at each meal. This is a product of papaya, and is an inexpensive means of replacing some digestive enzymes.

Enzymes from Food

Some enzymes can be "borrowed" by including cottage cheese, yogurt, or acidophilus in the diet. The bacteria in these foods produce some of the enzymes in which you may be deficient. The lactobacilli involved in the making of yogurt and cottage cheese produce lactase and other enzymes. They make these enzymes so they can break down lactose and other substrates for their own metabolism. The bacteria actually produce a slight excess of enzymes. An individual can take advantage of this excess by eating either cottage cheese or yogurt when he or she indulges in foods such as ice cream or fruits that contain lactose or fructose. The bacterial enzymes will digest a modest amount of these sugars when the individual may not have the enzymes to do the job alone.

Brewer's malt is rich in enzymes and may work well for some. Papayas and pineapple are other enzyme-rich foods one may try—remember, though, that they also contain fructose.

Unfriendly Bacteria

A myriad of tiny plants and animals normally inhabit the human colon. They are scavengers; they eat up the food nutrients that have not been assimilated in the digestive processes. From wasted food, these organisms provide heat and manufacture vital vitamins including vitamin K, essential to the body for blood clotting.

Among these miniature inhabitants are many species of bacteria. These include *E. coli*, the bacteroides family, *Streptococcus fecalis*, and *lactobacilli*. Most people harbor all of these and many, many more varieties. A number of molds and yeast also grow in the colon including *Candida albicans*.

The varieties of these bacteria are to a great extent controlled by what we eat. Some are favored by particular carbohydrates such as lactose, others may thrive on fat or protein. Some bacteria are potential enemies; when their numbers rise, the products of fermentation injure the bowel lining and cause diarrhea—irritable bowel disease.

Sometimes, the introduction of "stranger" bacteria is disastrous. Bacteria such as cholera, typhoid, shigella, staphylococci, and *E. coli* species can follow ingestion of spoiled or contaminated food or water.

Antibiotics can destroy the friendly bacteria and leave the harmful strains. What follows is an infection-caused irritable bowel condition that may be very serious. Usually, the upset results in a temporary irritable bowel disease that fades after a day or so. It may become chronic if sugars and fiber are eaten, thus enabling the offending bacteria to multiply. Infection injures the bowel lining so it no longer makes the enzymes necessary to digest such foods as lactose and fructose. The establishment of unfriendly bacteria becomes chronic, and in some cases of enterocolitis it may be life threatening. A very large percentage of irritable bowel disease begins with the taking of antibiotics for other problems.

One of the most friendly of bacteria is the lactobacillus. This is the bacteria that sours milk and makes kraut, yogurt, and cottage cheese. It is also the principal micro-inhabitant of the vagina. It keeps the vagina healthy by fermenting glycogen produced by mucous glands and makes the vaginal milieu acidic. This acid discourages the growth of yeast and undesirable bacterial organisms. We are introduced to this bacteria at birth. As we are born, nature wisely inoculates us with this tiny friend.

This organism can control what other bacteria grow by consuming all the food around. Including cottage cheese or yogurt in the diet daily helps keep the intestine planted with this friendly bacteria. Fostering a large number of these bacteria tends then to crowd out the less friendly organisms. As my wise farmer father would say, "The best way to control the weeds is to plant the wheat thick."

There is another benefit to managing the intestinal flora in this manner. The lactobacilli produce excess lactase and fructose aldolase. This may replace some of the enzyme you may lack, making you less intolerant of sugar. (If you are going to cheat with the diet and eat some ice cream or waffles and syrup, better follow up with some cottage cheese or yogurt along with potatoes or bread.) This is also a good way to combat infectious diarrhea; again, crowding out the weeds by planting the wheat thick.

Chapter 3

Diet and IBS Disorders

The Villains: Foods to Avoid

Fructose (Levulose)

Fructose intolerance has been the missing piece of the irritable bowel disease puzzle. The manifestations of fructose intolerance are nearly identical to those of lactose intolerance. The role of fructose in bowel disease has not been entertained in the past. Who would suspect that anything so wholesome as orange juice would be so devastating to the bowel lining as to destroy it and necessitate removal of the colon and the establishment of an ileostomy opening in the abdomen? Intolerance to this sugar has been the sleeper in the understanding of irritable bowel disease.

Fructose is the primary sweetener in honey, sweet fruits, and corn syrup or corn sweetener. It provides the sweetness to apples, pears, pineapples, peaches, dates, plums, melons, oranges, bananas, grapefruit, and others.

This sugar is now manufactured from corn. The corn is treated with enzymes to make synthetic honey called corn sweetener, corn syrup, or high fructose corn sweetener. Sometimes it is listed in food contents as sugar. It is a sugar, but since many people have fructose intolerance, it is hoped that foods made with this product will be accurately labeled. Corn syrup is a particularly insidious source of fructose, and is often simply called sugar on product labels. It is included in thousands of commercially produced foods such as ice cream, candy, waffle syrup, jams, jellies, glazes on bakery and cereal products, and soda pop.

Corn syrup is twice as sweet as cane or beet sugar (sucrose), and many times sweeter than lactose. This may be great for those who are weight conscious, as they need consume only half as many calories of this sugar to get the same sweetness as they would get using cane sugar. For most people, it is a perfectly acceptable food. Most people can convert fructose into glucose and assimilate it.

Not everyone with irritable bowel disease is intolerant of fructose. There are some who tolerate it well and others who have intolerance only when the bowel is acutely inflamed or irritated (as by lactose, sorbitol, mannitol, drugs, or infection).

Many people have tolerance to small amounts of fructose but have serious symptoms after large doses. The irritated bowel then fails to digest other foods such as lactose or wheat. As these foods fail to digest and be assimilated, they are fermented. Acids, alcohol, acetaldehyde, and gases resulting from the fermentation further irritate the bowel lining and impair digestion.

There is no product comparable to Lactaid or Lactrase for fructose intolerance. There is no specific enzyme supplement you can add to your diet that will facilitate the conversion of fructose to glucose. Supplementing your diet with lactobacilli from yogurt, cottage cheese, or acidophilus tablets may increase your fructose tolerance mildly.

Sorbitol and Mannitol

Humans were never equipped with the enzymes necessary to convert these alcohol sugars to glucose. They are not absorbed and remain in the intestine. Some intestinal bacteria are able to ferment them. Sorbitol occurs in apples, pears, and quinces; these cause gas in most people as the sorbitol is fermented.

These sugars are used in low-calorie and sugar-free candy and chewing gum and in some processed meats. Sorbitol is used as a laxative and mannitol is given intravenously as a diuretic to reduce brain swelling. (It is rapidly excreted by the kidneys; in the process it carries away significant amounts of water.)

In recent years, related nonabsorbed sugars have come into use for sweetening "sugar-free" foods and confections. Xylitol and maltitol are similar to sorbitol and mannitol. They are unabsorbed and fuel fermentation.

Large amounts of any of these sugars will cause irritable bowel disease.

Fiber

Despite what we are told by dieticians, gastroenterologists, herb wiccas, gynecologists, or chiropodists, fiber is not good for those of us with irritable bowel disease.

A half century ago, British surgeon, Dr. Dennis Burkitt went to Africa. While working as a missionary doctor, he noticed the virtual absence of irritable bowel disorders among the local people. They were also free of hemorrhoids, diabetes, gallstones, appendicitis, bowel cancer, and constipation. He attributed the intestinal health of these people to their diet that was high in fibrous barley bread. He then declared that the many ills of Western culture are caused by a lack of fiber in the diet, that white bread and sugar are the chief causes of most of humanity's intestinal ailments. The guru was believed, and his pronouncement soon became the untested canon of modern medicine. Not only has the Burkitt theory failed to prevent irritable bowel disease, the application of lots of fruits and fiber has actually made irritable bowel disease much worse, injuring many more than it has helped.

Since Dr. Burkitt's observation that the fiber-eating African natives rarely got bowel cancer, gallstones, appendicitis, hemorrhoids, or many other common gastrointestinal ailments, there has been a great interest in dietary fiber. The shelves of bookstores are crammed with diet books by self-styled "authorities," most of whom are on the fiber bandwagon. All kinds of great and wonderful things are touted by these fiber advocates. "Health food" suppliers push their fiber products.

One must be careful, however, in assigning explanations for observations such as absence of bowel cancer among African natives to fibrous barley bread. The observation that they do not get gastrointestinal diseases is probably valid. That fiber is the primary reason why is debatable and doubtful. It is equally true that their diets are low in lactose and fructose. The absence of these sugars accounts equally well for the rarity of intestinal problems. Although fiber may be protective, it is more likely that the absence of bowel cancer among the African natives is due to the absence of these sugars or animal proteins in their diets.

By definition, fiber consists of undigestible carbohydrates. That you and I cannot digest them does not mean that the yeasts and bacteria in the bowel cannot digest and ferment them. There is a level of fermentation in the colon that is normal. When the intestine is flooded with too much fermentable carbohydrates, intolerable amounts of the products of fermentation irritate the bowel lining and become absorbed into the blood to cause problems in the distant organs.

Many letters to the *Saturday Evening Post*'s Colitis Club and personal experience suggested that fiber is not kind to the irritable bowel. Fiber is composed of complex carbohydrates that are poorly digested. In many people, the poorly digested fiber causes the very same problems that poorly digested sugars cause; they ferment and produce gas, cramping, and diarrhea.

In one study, it was found that rats fed a wheat bran diet had significant intestinal bleeding. Wheat is the cause of colitis in celiac-sprue victims. (Their symptoms are indistinguishable from those who have colitis due to lactose or fructose intolerance. There is a considerable crossing-over effect, that is, celiac victims who are intolerant to wheat are often intolerant to lactose and fructose as well. Lactose or fructose intolerant individuals may have poor tolerance to wheat bran—particularly in large amounts.)

In spite of all the bad things said about refined and starchy foods, they have a certain beauty about them for persons with irritable bowel diseases. Cane sugar, white bread, and potatoes are all converted to glucose and absorbed into the blood rapidly and quite completely. This leaves little residue to pass into the lower digestive tract to ferment. (One study showed that mashed potatoes raises blood glucose levels almost as quickly as sugar itself. This suggested that the conversion of potato starch to glucose and its absorption takes place very rapidly.) If fiber causes you to have colitis symptoms, it is best to avoid it. Brown bread is perhaps a little more nutritious than white, but if it causes bowel irritation, then white bread is far better for you. Do not feel you must slavishly obey all the rules of all the experts—including this one. Find what works for you. This book is meant to be used as a guide for a rational approach to finding the foods responsible for your irritable bowel disease.

Beans

Beans are likely to cause problems for those with irritable bowel problems beyond the socially embarrassing production of intestinal gas. (Gas production by any food raises the suspicion flag that it may be irritating to the sensitive gastrointestinal tract.)

Most beans contain an enzyme that blocks the digestion of starches by amylase. (This blocker enzyme was briefly marketed a few years ago as a weight control aid.) The action of this substance permits starches to pass undigested into the lower intestine where bacteria ferment them. In addition to the gas, the fermentation yields irritating chemicals including alcohol, acetaldehyde, and lactic, acetic, and propionic acids.

The amount of gas produced by beans is inversely proportional to how much they are cooked. Very thoroughly cooking destroys the starch blocker. Lightly cooked beans are likely to contain significant starch blocker and cause much gas to be produced and some irritating chemicals.

Friendly Foods

Sucrose

Common table sugar is sucrose. Cane and beet sugars are sucrose. It is used in coffee, home cooking, canning, bakery items, and candy making. This is a natural sugar separated from the pulp of plants. It is "refined" in the sense that impurities have been removed, but it is nonetheless a natural sugar. (The only differences between beet and cane sugars are the trace impurities in each.) Generally, sucrose in small amounts is tolerated by irritable bowel victims, although there are rare instances of sucrose intolerance.

Like lactose, sucrose is a disaccharide. This means its molecule is formed by the joining together of two molecules of simple sugars. In sucrose, one molecule is glucose and the second fructose. One would anticipate irritable bowel problems from the fructose and also because it requires two steps in its digestion: (1) the separation of the glucose and fructose and (2) the conversion of the fructose to glucose. Almost all people have the enzymes necessary to separate sucrose into its simple sugars. Just why the fructose portion of sucrose does not cause more bowel irritation is unclear; an educated guess is that as sucrose is hydrolyzed (the process of separating the glucose from the fructose), the conversion of the fructose to glucose is in some way facilitated. (Fructose, lactose, sucrose, and starch are all converted to glucose before the body uses them for fuel.) Because sucrose is a source of fructose, those with irritable bowel disease should use it with caution.

According to the Food and Drug Administration (FDA), the word sugar is supposed to indicate sucrose when it is used in product ingredient lists. Unfortunately, this is not strictly enforced. Many manufacturers list sugar as an ingredient when they are actually using corn sweetener. Strictly speaking, corn sweetener is sugar, but in view of the discovery that the fructose in corn sweetener causes irritable bowel syndrome, regulations requiring corn sweetener to be listed on labels as such must be enforced. The Food and Drug Administration has been informed of this problem. It will take the letters of many individuals who have fructose intolerance to spur the FDA to take action.

Glucose (Dextrose)

Glucose is the gasoline of the human body. It is the fuel the machine was designed to run on. It is actively absorbed from the digestive system. Glucose absorption begins in the mouth. When we speak of blood sugar, we are talking about glucose in the blood. Glucose is a particularly attractive fuel. It burns cleanly into carbon dioxide and water. The products of its combustion are harmless to all tissues. There are no waste residues that may accumulate in the body. Brain cells burn only glucose as fuel. This places these cells at risk for deprivation of fuel. Serious injury results when the brain is deprived of this fuel for even a few minutes. When the blood sugar is too low, seizures and coma result. Brain cells benefit from this fuel selectivity as the lack of residue in its combustion allows the cells to function often for more than a hundred years! Impaired burning of glucose occurs in diabetes; the sugar then accumulates in the blood and spills into the urine.

Because glucose is so rapidly absorbed by the intestine, none of it reaches the lower bowel where the destructive fermentation of irritable bowel diseases play.

Glucose is the most common sugar in nature, but it seldom occurs in simple form. More commonly it occurs as long chains in starch or cellulose. (Wood is almost entirely glucose chains.) Starch and cellulose are formed by removing water from glucose.

Starch

The human body was designed to use starch as its principal fuel source. Starch is concentrated glucose. The long chains of glucose are broken down into free glucose that enters the energy cycle of metabolism. For the body there is an advantage in using starch as opposed to free glucose. The digestive process breaks the starch down slowly, feeding glucose into the blood over a long period of time. Straight glucose enters the blood all at once, raising the blood sugar to levels that may cause spillage into the urine (diabetes).

Starch is not absorbed into the blood as such; it must first be changed to glucose. The digestive process involves the adding of water to starches and reconverting them into glucose. Humans are not equipped to digest cellulose, which is made of longer, more complicated chains of glucose that we call fiber (see Figure 3.1).

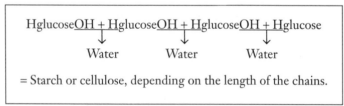

Figure 3.1 Starch formation.

Artificial Sweetening Agents

Artificial sweetening agents fall into two categories:

1. The nonabsorbable sugars already mentioned— sorbitol, mannitol, xylitol, and maltitol. These are

not friends. They are really indigestible sugars, and the label "sugarless" is technically fraudulent. These sugars are important because they are extremely irritating to the sensitive bowel. There is a dose relationship for these irritants: the larger the dose the greater the degree of irritation. As with the other poorly absorbed sugars, small amounts may be tolerated, but they should be religiously avoided when the bowel is irritated.

2. The synthetic chemical sweeteners—saccharin, cyclamate, asulfame, and aspartame (NutraSweet). Cyclamate has been removed from the market, probably wrongfully. The other agents are tolerated well by the irritable bowel. Hence one may drink diet soda pop all day with no untoward effects to the bowel. The amount of these substances used is very small because they are so potent in imparting the sweet taste. The use of artificial sweeteners is recommended particularly in soda pop and foods that would normally be sweetened with corn sweetener. The long-term effects of these agents are unknown. There is cause for some concern with aspartame. Aspartame is made by joining two amino acids (protein building blocks) with a molecule of wood alcohol. Wood alcohol metabolizes into formaldehyde, or embalming fluid. (The propionate used as a preservative in bread also breaks down into formaldehyde.) There is no indication of acute

injury with tiny amounts of these sweeteners. It may take years to notice any accumulative injury. For the moment, they are a boon to irritable bowel sufferers.

Potatoes

Among the best friends of the irritable bowel is the potato. Potatoes are easily digested, and their starch turned to glucose that is quickly absorbed. Many with irritable bowel disease, particularly those in the older age brackets, are taking diuretic drugs (water pills) for high blood pressure or heart disease. Diuretics cause increased water to pass from the body by getting rid of salt. As the salt is removed from the blood by the kidneys, water is carried out along with it. This is the desired effect of the drugs. Unfortunately, potassium is excreted along with the sodium salt. This may dangerously deplete body potassium and serious, even fatal, disturbance of the heart's rhythm may result.

To prevent potassium depletion, potassium pills are often prescribed for those on diuretic medications. Orange juice and bananas are also recommended as a source of additional potassium, but these often aggravate irritable bowel disease. Not mentioned is the potato! These are particularly kind to irritated digestive systems and a baked potato has a potassium content of 782 milligrams, while the orange has only 496 and the banana 440.

Why a baked potato? All of the compounds of potassium are highly soluble in water. When potatoes (or any other fruit or vegetable) are boiled, much of the potassium leaches out into the water and is often poured off (water-soluble B vitamins are lost in the same manner).

Baked or steamed potatoes are an excellent source of potassium for those in need of additional amounts of this vital mineral and particularly for those with irritable bowel disease. Tomatoes are another excellent source of potassium for irritable bowel sufferers. They are also a source of vitamin C equal to oranges.

Protein

Protein-rich foods are friendly to victims of irritable bowel disease. There are two reasons for this. First, few bacteria are able to break down protein and ferment it. Hence undigested protein that reaches the lower digestive tract is not fermented to any significant extent.

The second reason has to do with the chemical properties of sols and gels. Sols are compounds that are highly soluble in water; sugar and salt are examples of sols. The breakdown products of carbohydrates tend to form sols, which tend to make liquid stools.

Gels are only partially soluble in water. Jello is an example of a gel. When the water/Jello mix is warm, or there is an excess of water, the mix behaves as a liquid.

When cooled or when water is removed, a semisolid results. When proteins are broken down by digestion, small elements of the protein are released into the intestine. Here they tend to form more solid stools. Cheese is particularly noted for forming solid stools; it is because of the formation of gel.

Jello has been a standard treatment for infant diarrhea. The notion is sound enough, but it does not work. There is so much sugar in Jello that the sugar sols overwhelm the gel formation. Not understanding this we have made the illnesses of multitudes of infants worse by giving them Jello.

In the digestive process, some of the protein is converted into glucose.

Fats

Like proteins, fats are well tolerated by irritable bowels. Undigested fats contribute little to intestinal fermentation. Much of the fat consumed, particularly fats from animal sources, comes in the form of triglyceride. Three molecules of fatty acid are joined to one molecule of glycerol. The enzyme lipase splits the fatty acids away from the glycerol.

Fats are very poorly soluble in water and are extremely weak acids. Because of their very low solubility (fats would rather dissolve in organic solvents such as ether or gasoline), there is normally a heavy wastage. Much of the insoluble fat remains in the food stream and is passed in the stool.

One can reduce the amount of fat absorbed in the intestine with calcium supplements (more on the advantages of calcium for IBS sufferers in the following section.) Calcium combines with fatty acids to make an insoluble soap that cannot be absorbed into the blood.

The Calcium Paradox

Historically, kidney-stone formers have been cautioned to avoid hard water, calcium supplements, and dairy foods because the calcium in them would contribute to kidney stones. Reason would suggest this to be the case. It has been feared that excess calcium would cause the formation of calcium oxalate stones. This fear presents a particular problem for women who are advised to take calcium supplements to avoid osteoporosis. Are you causing kidney stones by taking calcium supplements to avoid osteoporosis?

In the section on kidney stones, it was pointed out that in irritable bowel disease excessive calcium is absorbed from the intestine, which then overloads the kidneys' excretory ability. Reason would recommend against putting large amounts of calcium into a leaky system that will allow too much of the element into the blood.

In chapter 5, a calcium supplement of 1 gram of calcium carbonate per fat-bearing meal is recommended as a measure to control weight by preventing fat absorption. Is there a hazard in taking what amounts to a large amount of calcium? Are calcium supplements courting danger? Will they cause kidney stones?

The answer is no. Paradoxically, the calcium supplements are more likely to prevent kidney stones than to cause them because a large amount of calcium carbonate will block its own absorption. A calcium supplement of this magnitude will decrease the acidity of the bowel contents. As the acidity of the bowel decreases (even by a small increment), the solubility of calcium diminishes sharply and insoluble calcium cannot be absorbed. (You cannot make the contents of the bowel too alkaline with calcium carbonate either, because it becomes insoluble and inert near neutral pH.) You cannot cause excessive calcium absorption by taking calcium carbonate (though it may be possible with some other salts of calcium). The best protection from excess calcium absorption is the avoidance of food elements that ferment and produce acid in the intestines.

Appearing in the May 1986 issue of *Consult* was an excellent review article by Dr. Alan G. Wasserstein, assistant professor of medicine at the University of Pennsylvania School of Medicine. In the article, Dr. Wasserstein made some important points:

In the intestinal lumen, calcium and oxalate form an insoluble and poorly absorbed complex. When free calcium in the intestinal lumen decreases, free oxalate increases, and so does the absorption of such oxalate . . . restricting dietary calcium may do more harm than good if it results in increased urinary oxalate excretion. A small increase in such urine oxalate excretion could enhance stone formation more than would a large increase in urinary calcium excretion. . . . Treat hyper-oxaluria by restricting dietary oxalate and increasing calcium intake. This should help to prevent calcium stone formation. . . . A calcium carbonate supplement of 1.3 grams twice a day . . . usually effectively reduces urine oxalate excretion by patients with enteric hyperoxaluria. There is little risk of exacerbating stone formation by engendering hypercalciuria because such patients tend to absorb calcium poorly and they excrete little of it.

His point is that the kidneys can excrete large amounts of calcium in the absence of oxalate. Tiny amounts of oxalate can initiate calcium kidney-stone formation. Calcium supplements bind oxalate in the intestine so it passes in the stool and never reaches the kidneys.

A reason for those with irritable bowel disease to take calcium supplements is suggested by Dr. Martin Lipkin of the Memorial Sloan-Kettering Cancer Center in New York City, who reported findings that calcium supplements may significantly reduce the chances of developing cancer of the colon in irritable bowel patients in the *New*

England Journal of Medicine (313:22, 1381, 1985). Ten patients at risk for a type of colon cancer that tends to run in families were studied by researchers from the Memorial Sloan-Kettering Cancer Center and from Cornell University, New York. None of the patients had cancer, but the cells in the linings of their colons were growing much more rapidly than normal. (Cells of the bowel lining, like the cells of the skin, are being constantly replaced. Irritation of the bowel lining greatly speeds the process.) This cell proliferation may be an indication of likely cancer development. After taking 1,250 milligrams of calcium a day (approximately the recommended minimal daily allowance for adults) in the form of calcium carbonate for two to three months, colon cell growth in these patients was reduce to more normal levels. This reduction in cell proliferation may also mean a reduction in the risk of cancer for these patients.

Five Reasons for IBS Sufferers to Take Calcium

1. Calcium supplements reduce the acidity of the food stream in the intestines. Excess lactic and acetic acids in the bowel severely irritate the bowel lining. Calcium combines with these acids and precipitates, making them harmless. By neutralizing the acidity of the bowel contents, calcium limits is own absorption. (Calcium does not neutralize

alcohol and acetaldehyde that are equally irritating and harmful to the delicate intestinal membranes. You cannot take calcium and forget about the avoidance of fermentable sugars.)

2. Calcium supplements help to soap out excess bile acid. The supplements will materially reduce blood cholesterol by eliminating the body's greatest source of this unwanted material: reabsorbed bile acid. Free bile is itself irritating to the intestinal lining, which creates a laxative effect. Calcium is constipating because it removes this irritant.

3. Calcium supplements help to soap out excessive fat from dietary sources. This is important for weight control. People with irritable bowel diseases tend to absorb fat excessively and become hopelessly obese. These individuals have great difficulty keeping off unwanted fat once they lose it. Calcium blocks the absorption of fat.

4. By raising the pH (reducing the acidity), calcium supplements help to greatly reduce the absorption of unwanted metals (aluminum, lead, mercury, and cadmium).

5. Calcium supplements probably reduce one's chances for bowel cancer by reducing cellular proliferation caused by irritation of the lining membranes.

Are All Calcium Supplements Created Equal?

Many ask if it matters what kind of calcium supplements they take. Calcium is calcium, but there are differences in formulations of the different products. Many calcium supplements are sweetened with sorbitol or mannitol and are highly disturbing to the irritable bowel.

Calcium carbonate has the highest calcium content per gram of tablet. The lactate, gluconate, citrate, and phosphate compounds of calcium all have heavier components making up the noncalcium portion of the preparation. These are generally more expensive and have no advantage over calcium carbonate.

Oyster shells are a favorite source of calcium carbonate. The oyster actually purifies the calcium. It selectively puts calcium into its shell, rejecting contaminants such as lead that occur in other sources such as dolomite.

Bone meal is an easily available source of calcium, but bones tend to contain lead (from air and water contamination caused by the burning of leaded fuels by automobiles). Lead causes problems for the body because, in many instances, the body mistakes lead for calcium and incorporates it in bones and enzymes, thus making enzymes that do not work. Bone meal produces calcium phosphate. Phosphate causes increased work for the kidneys and tends to carry more calcium away from the body in the stool than calcium phosphate provides. Pregnant women get leg cramps from calcium deficiency after taking calcium phosphate or drinking a quart of milk a day. (Milk may rob you of more calcium than it provides! This is because of its very high phosphate content. Phosphate carries calcium with it when it is excreted.) Diuretics cause excretion of calcium as well as sodium and potassium. They too may provoke leg cramps by causing a mild calcium deficiency.

The Truth About Cholesterol

In the 1950s, simple chemical analysis of the waxy material in atherosclerotic plaques of diseased arteries yielded cholesterol. Since then, "cholesterol" has been a dirty word. People were cautioned not to eat eggs, as they contained cholesterol. So for thirty years, "eggs" has also been a dirty word.

As a student of chemistry, I have been amazed at my profession's ignorance of chemistry. (Doctors as a group abhor chemistry though, ultimately, life depends on a normal sequence of chemical reactions.) Cholesterol is a wax that is closely related to parafin. I have been baffled and perplexed by the readiness of the medical profession and the public to accept the idea that cholesterol is absorbed from the diet into the blood. Cholesterol simply will not dissolve in water (the acid form of cholesterol, cholic acid, is soluble). Because of this, I have been a closet doubter regarding the theory that cholesterol in the diet plays a significant role in human disease or nutrition. In recent years (in very tiny print), the medical establishment has confessed that, in tests, it could not trace labeled cholesterol from eggs in the human bloodstream.

Cholesterol has its origin in the sex hormones and the hormones of the cortisone family. The respective glands produce these hormones, and they would accumulate forever but for the liver. The liver breaks the hormones down to their parent molecule: cholesterol. The cholesterol is partially broken down further when the alcohol group on the cholesterol is oxidized to an organic acid. This is comparable to the oxidation of cider to hard cider (alcoholic) and then to vinegar (acid). The acid form of cholesterol (cholic acid) is excreted into the bile. This form of cholesterol is water soluble. In the intestine, cholic acid appears to that organ to be a food fatty acid. The cholic acid is absorbed and sent back to the liver; the liver rejects it, putting it back into the bile. This has the potential for a vicious cycle.

Hence, the body manufactures its cholesterol. Cholesterol is an essential constituent of the brain. It is also the chassis or chemical frame the sex hormones and cortisone are built on. In the late 1960s, a chemical was marketed that blocked cholesterol production. (It was sold under the name of MER-29.) After two years, many of those taking the drug suffered degeneration of the brain. Taking drugs to reduce cholesterol should be viewed with caution and suspicion.

The body excretes cholesterol in the bile as cholic acid (cholesterol acid). It is secreted as the sodium or potassium salts (soaps). These substances are soluble in water and act as detergents in spreading the digestive juices throughout the food stream. In colitis, these salts tend to be reabsorbed excessively as evidenced by the high rate of gallstone formation. After reabsorption, they are removed from the blood by the liver and re-excreted in the bile. The repeated absorption and excretion overloads the biliary system, putting excessive bile salt in the available biliary fluid. Precipitation takes place in the supersaturated bile, and cholesterol biliary stones form. The process also causes high blood levels of cholesterol.

Cholic acid reabsorption can be blocked with calcium supplements. Calcium combines with the cholic acid and forms an insoluble soap that passes in the stool. Studies have shown calcium supplements to be highly effective in lowering cholesterol.

Calcium supplements and the treatment of irritable bowel disease may prove to be the best way to prevent atherosclerosis.

Chapter 4

The Self-Help Way to Treat Colitis and Other IBS Disorders

The Ulcerative Colitis/Irritable Bowel Diet

The goal of this diet is to sharply limit the amount of poorly assimilated sugars and fiber that may ferment in the bowel and cause gas, diarrhea, and irritation. These sugars are: fructose, found in fruit and fruit juices; honey and corn sweetener; lactose, found in milk; sorbitol and mannitol, used in sugar-free products; and wheat-bran fiber.

Fructose foods to be avoided:

- Orange juice or any sweet fruits including oranges, apples, pears, grapes, bananas, pineapple, and melons.

- honey, jams, or jellies
- waffle syrup made with corn sweetener
- corn sweetener (in soda pop, pastries, candy, cereals, coffee creamers, salad dressing, sweet pickles, ice cream, ham, and so forth). Read the labels on all foods.

Lactose foods to be avoided:

- milk
- chocolate milk
- ice cream
- whey

Butter and cheese are permitted as the lactose has been removed in their production. Cottage cheese and yogurt are permitted as most of the lactose has been removed by the fermentation involved in their production.

Sorbitol- and mannitol-containing foods to be avoided:

- "sugarless" chewing gum
- candy (such as diabetic candy)
- toothpaste
- breath mints
- some processed meats, which may contain these sugars

Foods permitted:

- rice and corn cereals
- white bread
- cheese
- butter
- meat, fish, and poultry
- well-cooked eggs
- all vegetables except sweet corn
  and dried beans
- tomatoes
- avocados
- very small amounts of cane sugar
- drink at least six glasses of water each day.

How the Diet Works

Irritable bowel disease and its arthritis most often occur in individuals who lack some of the enzymes necessary to digest certain sugars and fiber. As these undigested carbohydrates remain in the intestine, they are fermented by the bacterial and yeast inhabitants of the bowel. This produces large volumes of gas, alcohol, and lactic and acetic acids, plus a myriad of other chemical products such as acetaldehyde that irritate the bowel locally and are absorbed into the blood and circulated to cause disease in distant organs such as eyes, joints, skin, liver, and kidneys.

The sugars that frequently fail to be digested are:

1. Fructose is the natural sugar in sweet fruits and honey and is also found in a synthetic source, corn sweetener. Many people are unable to convert it into glucose for absorption into the blood. Fructose intolerance has not been appreciated as a cause of serious health problems until now. It appears to be the sleeper that has been missed as a causative factor in irritable bowel disease. Recent studies show it to be the most important factor causing bowel irritation, which in turn causes arthritis. Individuals may be intolerant of either fructose or lactose or both, particularly when their irritable bowel disease is active.

2. Lactose is the natural sugar in milk. It has long been observed that many adults do not tolerate lactose well.

3. Sorbitol and mannitol are used in so-called sugar-free foods such as diabetic candy, chewing gum, toothpaste, and breath mints. These sugars are not converted to glucose and absorbed by humans. They stay in the intestine where bacteria metabolize them and form irritating chemicals. Hence all people are intolerant of them, and substantial

amounts of these sugars will cause irritable bowel disease in virtually anyone. They must be avoided scrupulously by those with irritable bowel disease.

4. Fiber foods such as wheat bran and beans cause the same problems for the irritable bowel that poorly absorbed sugars cause. Fiber is not digested and absorbed, hence it adds to the fermentation process in the intestine. Fiber is not essential in the diet, particularly if you have irritable bowel problems. (The National Cancer Institute's assertion that fiber prevents cancer is based on the flimsiest of evidence. There is strong evidence, however, that irritable bowel disease does predispose one to bowel cancer.)

How to Use the Diet

The colitis diet is admittedly spartan, but following it is a small price to pay for relief from the pain, inconvenience, danger, and embarrassment of colitis. When an individual is having severe or acute symptoms such as frequent diarrhea and passage of mucus, blood, or pus, I recommend following the diet in all details. If the sufferer is having only minor symptoms such as gas or pruritus, he can experiment a little to determine whether he is intolerant of fructose, lactose, or both.

Assuming the worst, one may start the day with a break-fast of ham, bacon, or sausage; white toast with butter; puffed rice or Rice Krispies (with water or soy milk and a touch of sugar). Later, when symptoms subside, one may find he or she is tolerant of lactose, then milk may be used. Eggs may be eaten—fried, poached, boiled, or scrambled (it is very important they be cooked thoroughly; eggs contain a virus that causes cancer in chickens). Drink a glass of tomato juice. Wheat bran cereals must be avoided as well as whole wheat bread or toast.

For lunch, any of the meats may be eaten: fish, chicken, pork, or beef. Rice, steamed vegetables (except sweet corn and dried beans), potatoes prepared in any fashion, cooked green beans, any soup, and sugar-free dessert may be had.

Dinner may include any of the above foods. A sample meal may consist of one or two cheese sandwiches that may be toasted, macaroni and cheese, or a meat dish. Once a day, a serving of cottage cheese or yogurt should be eaten to control the bacterial population in the intestine. Potatoes may be included, canned beets, carrots, peas, string beans, frozen (then cooked) vegetables such as peas, beans, broccoli, brussels sprouts, cauliflower, carrots, and canned vegetables with the exception of corn and beans. Coffee, tea, or diet pop may be used as desired provided they are not sweetened with fructose or sorbitol.

Hot spicy foods such as Mexican, Indian curries, pizza, and chili are to be carefully avoided. Chocolate bothers many and should be avoided. When eating out, hamburgers, cheeseburgers, fish-fillet sandwiches, chicken sandwiches, chicken, french fries, potatoes and meat, coffee, and diet pop are all allowed in the diet. It is probably worthwhile to take a multivitamin supplement with the diet as it tends to be low on vitamins, particularly vitamin C. It also tends to be high in fat. I suggest one or two Tums with fatty meals to absorb the fat before you do. Lettuce can be a problem for some, particularly those suffering from diverticular disease. Most notice improvement on this regimen within two or three days.

Chapter 5

Weight Loss for IBS Sufferers

I ndividuals with irritable bowel disease have impaired digestion. However in one respect, their digestive systems seem to work too well: in the absorption of fat.

As a young country doctor, I doubted the veracity of my many obese middle-aged patients who insisted they gained weight in spite of eating very sparingly. I now recognize that this is often true. Another doubter reported in the *British Medical Journal* (292:983–987) that, contrary to expectations, obese women had higher rates of metabolism than matched thin women. This shattered the theory that the obese became fat because they do not burn calories as rapidly as lean persons. There are factors involved that appear to contradict the accepted concept of energy balance: when you expend more energy than you consume in food you lose weight, and when you eat more than you burn, you gain weight. Some gain weight while others do not when they eat the same amount of food. This suggests that some people extract many more calories from their diets than others. This is particularly true for women. One of the effects of the hormone estrogen is the deposition of fat. Animal feeders give their animals estrogen to make them gain more weight.

Because many who suffer from irritable bowel disease have associated weight problems, some suggestions for weight control are offered here. Those with severe diarrhea suffer marked malabsorption and are underweight and malnourished. Since the food stream passes through so fast, few of the nutrients are absorbed. For these people, good nutrition depends on alleviating the irritation of the intestine so it may perform its absorptive functions.

Many more individuals having less severe colitis suffer hyperabsorption of fats, bile acids, calcium, and metals. For them, obesity is the problem. They gain weight even while eating very carefully. These victims try many weight-loss programs, but none are successful. Starvation-type diets allow them to lose a little weight, but it always comes back almost immediately.

One insight comes from the truism that farmers have long known: "You cannot fatten hogs on wheat." Wheat has a high starch content, but is very low in fat. Corn, on the other hand, has a fairly high fat content. Thus to fatten hogs, you must provide them with preformed fat! In recent years, researchers have arrived at the same conclusion about the human body. It, too, is very poor at turning carbohydrates into fat. This observation has tremendous implications for irritable bowel sufferers. It suggests that the fat accumulated in the body is fat that has been eaten, not fat that has been converted from carbohydrates or proteins. You do not become fat from eating carbohydrates but from eating fats. In mild irritable bowel disease, fats are absorbed excessively. Carbohydrates do play a key role, however. The body preferentially burns carbohydrates. Thus carbohydrates protect the fat from being burned—and you do not lose weight.

Considerations for Would-be Dieters

Exercise Alone May Not Be the Best Way to Lose Weight

There is a fundamental law of physics that operates in nature. It is a law like the law of gravity in that it cannot be broken. This law states that a small amount of heat energy transforms into a large amount of mechanical motion energy.

An illustration of this law is the burning of a gallon of gasoline. It is able to push a four-thousand-pound automobile for twenty miles! Incredible, is it not? Remember, this law is unbreakable. What it means to you is that, if you are trying to lose weight, a pound of fat (which is as energy-laden as gasoline) can propel your body "twenty miles" or more, whether you choose to run or walk.

Translated into practical terms, it means that exercise may be the best way, but it is a very hard way, to lose weight (and probably not a very pleasant one either). In the first place, if you were athletically inclined and enjoyed prolonged walking or running, you would not have the weight problem you are presently concerned about. Sadly, too, walking is a very efficient expenditure of energy. You get a great many miles on that pound of fat (thirteen is the generally accepted mileage from a pound of fat). While it is true that you do lose weight through exercise, and the exercise is good for you in other ways, it is not a fast, easy way to lose weight.

What about exercise machines and appliances? They are great if they get you to exercise, but they will not bring about any rapid weight loss. Nearly all the gadgets advertised for losing weight are gimmicks and are generally useless. The thirteen miles of exercise per pound of fat applies no matter how you choose to do the exercise. Do not let this excuse you from exercising; for many reasons exercise is important for your health—it is just not an easy way to lose weight.

Basal Metabolism

To maintain life, there must be a continuous expenditure of energy. The maintenance of heartbeat, respiratory muscle action, digestion, muscle tone, and body heat requires a constant utilization of heat energy. This is called basal metabolism. When a person does not eat, calories of stored energy (fat and protein) are burned. (This is like tearing up the boxcars for fuel to keep the locomotive running.) A second unbreakable law in nature states that if you do not eat, you must lose weight. This is the weight of the fuel used from body stores. If you wish to lose weight, all you have to do is eat less. It has been determined that a pound of fat is equivalent to about 3,600 calories. Thus, if you burn 2,000 calories in a day and eat 2,000 calories, you neither gain nor lose weight. If you burn 2,000 calories a day and eat 2,600 calories in a day, the extra 600 calories per day for a week will cause you to gain about one pound. If you burn 2,000 calories per day and eat only 1,400 calories, the daily deficit of 600 calories will cause you to burn off a pound of fat per week. If you wish to lose more, you must curtail eating even more (600 calories a day is the amount of food equivalent to nine slices of bread).

The energy needs of different individuals vary greatly. The lumberjack may require 7,000 or 8,000 calories per day to maintain a stable weight. The octogenarian who lies in bed most of the time may maintain weight on as little as 800 calories a day. Generally, a large person will expend more calories than a small one. The stevedore who burns 6,000 calories a day can eat 2,000 calories a day and still lose a pound a day, while the 105-pound secretary who expends 1,200 calories a day cannot lose a pound by starving in less than three days! Practically speaking then, if you wish to lose weight, you must sharply reduce the amount of food you eat daily. If you reduce your food intake, your basal metabolism will bring about a weight loss—all you have to do is sit back and let it happen. Pushing yourself away from the table may be the most effective exercise you can do to lose weight.

Reducing Food Intake

Most people overeat because they are anxious, not because they are hungry. Food is a very potent tranquilizer (very pleasant, too), and has a calming effect on the nervous system. The kind of food eaten is less of a factor in allaying anxiety than the bulk, the timeliness, and the act of eating. Thus, you can satisfy this anxiety-driven desire to eat with foods that are low in calories just as well as you can with ones that are high in calories. So have lots of low calorie foods at hand to eat for the alleviation of anxiety. Diet soda pop is such a "food." It is filling and you think you are getting something when, in fact, you are getting only colored water. Celery sticks, radishes, and carrot sticks are good ways to fill your need for "tranquilization" food.

In trying to cut down on your food consumption remember: It is easier to resist temptation on the supermarket shelf than to resist it on the refrigerator shelf. If you want to lose weight, the most effective action is not to bring all the goodies home from the store. Then when you feel the urge to eat, you will satisfy it with tomatoes, celery, and diet pop.

There is a great difference in the caloric content of different foods. Fats and oils have the most calories per gram or pound. If you wish to lose weight, you must cut down sharply on fatty foods: meats, butter, pastries, etc. Breads, potatoes, and cereals are fairly high in calories, and we tend to eat rather large quantities of these. To lose weight, these foods must be curbed. Fresh vegetables commonly used in salads tend to be low in calories. To satisfy your need for food and bulk, you can still lose weight by increasing the amount of these foods while decreasing the fats and carbohydrates.

Daily Weight Fluctuations

A day-to-day weight variation of three or found pounds is quite normal. This weight variation is due to water retention and is temporary. High intake of salt causes water to be retained; it is shed later as the salt is removed from the body by the kidneys. Surprisingly small amounts of salt will cause a disturbingly large water accumulation. This water retention is of the order of nine pounds of water for one teaspoon of salt! It is very easy to gain four or five pounds after one salty meal (note: you do not have to eat four or five pounds of food to gain five pounds).

Don't Lose Weight Too Rapidly

Because of the physical, chemical, and health laws involved, it is unrealistic to expect very rapid weight loss
by any safe means. A pound-per-week loss is significant,
and no one should be discouraged that he or she is not
losing more rapidly. Total starvation will cause weight
losses of up to a pound per day, but starvation beyond a
few days results in severe ketoacidosis that may predispose one to infections and other health hazards.

Commercial Diet Plans

Food supplements or replacements such as Slim Fast or
Sustacal have been designed to provide the body's needs
for vitamins, minerals, and protein with minimal calories.
Usually they recommend substituting a can of the product for each of two meals every day and having one small,
balanced meal of food. This makes for a diet of about one
thousand calories per day that can be followed for a prolonged period of time without danger of malnutrition or
ketoacidosis. Many other weight-loss programs lack the
feature of maintaining protein balance and avoiding ketosis built into the diets. The plans work for many. Too
often, the products are taken with meals rather than instead of them. In this case, they do no good.

Weight reduction clubs such as Weight Watchers and TOPS are helpful in motivating you to adhere to the dietary restraints and exercising needed to lose weight and keep it off.

What about diet pills—the easy quick fix? Every day millions of Americans visit their physicians and ask for diet pills with the anticipation that taking them will make them lose weight. Do they really work? They work only if they cause you to eat less. If they do not, they are useless. These drugs are powerful stimulants. (Many are related to the street drug "speed.") They have a side effect of depressing the appetite. It is for this side effect that people take them. The drugs do not cause any weight loss directly, but they may curb your appetite so you eat less. The weight loss comes only from eating less, not from the action of the pills. One only needs to remember the recent introduction of the drug Fen-Phen, which was withdrawn from the market because it was found to be causing heart damage, to realize that many drugs have long-term damaging results, many of which are still unknown. Overall, the drug treatment of obesity has been rather disappointing except to the drug companies.

Many people go to their doctors and ask for water pills to help them lose weight. Diuretics cause a rapid loss of two to four pounds—of water. They do not cause any loss of fat. The sudden weight loss tickles the vanity but, in a day or two, most of the water is replaced and the weight returns to its original value.

Talk to Your Doctor

A programmed weight loss of more than ten pounds should be undertaken only under medical supervision. Marked changes in exercise and diet may impose problems on latent diabetics or on individuals with unrecognized anemia and heart or kidney disease. Those who are overweight because of underactive thyroid glands may starve and exercise, and still lose little due to their very low basal metabolism. For them, weight control may be brought about by correcting the thyroid abnormality.

The Truth About Ketogenic Diets

A ketogenic, short-cut diet that involves partial starvation by excluding all carbohydrates will result in a rapid weight loss of up to a pound per day by forcing the body to burn its fat. This is not a healthy diet, and it should not be used unless one is in good health and then for no longer than a month. Carbohydrates (sugars and starches) are the "gasoline" the body was designed to run on. Just as an auto can be forced to run on gasoline substitutes (usually very inefficiently), the body can be forced to run on fat and protein. When carbohydrates are completely denied, the body can strip the nitrogen from amino acids (the building blocks of protein). This provides a considerable source of carbohydrate to operate on for a while—but at the expense of muscle loss. The goal is to get rid of the fat, not the muscles. When this source of energy is depleted, the fat stores are burned.

Curiously, in this starvation situation, fat does not burn efficiently. Like burning damp leaves, there is more smoke than flame produced. The inefficiently burned fat forms soluble unburned intermediates that are passed in the urine and breath. (These make the peculiar breath odor common to extremely ill persons whose metabolism is in a state of starvation.) This situation is called ketoacidosis. With keto acids being excreted in the urine and through the lungs, there is a rapid weight loss by this wastage of fat. A person in ketoacidosis will lose about a pound a day. While ketosis causes a rapid weight loss, it is not a healthy state. As noted previously, it is not recommended for anyone not in good health or beyond a month at a time. A high-protein intake is suggested during a ketogenic diet to protect muscle proteins as much as possible. A ketogenic, quick weight-loss diet is listed on page 126.

Recent studies have indicated that the human animal does not readily change carbohydrate into fat. This is an important principle. It means that the fats you deposit in your body come from fats you consume, not from fats made from carbohydrates.

Because the body preferentially burns carbohydrates, dietary sugar and starch prevent the burning of fat stores. There is a relationship between obesity and carbohydrate excess. Carbohydrates protect fat stores. The most rapid means of losing weight is the ketogenic diet—the elimination of all carbohydrates from the diet. This forces the body to burn stored fat. The rapid weight-loss diet that follows is based on this principle. On this diet, I was able to lose five pounds of weight a week while eating a pound of Kentucky Fried Chicken a day!

This diet tends to be a high-protein diet, and a discussion of protein's role is important: whereas carbohydrates and fat are primarily energy resources, protein is the body's main structural material. Proteins are long chains of amino acids that in many ways resemble the long chains of glucose that make up starches and fiber. They differ in that the individual links in the protein chains vary considerably. There are about twenty different amino acids, and the various proteins are made up of these amino acids in different sequences, whereas starches and fiber are made up of only glucose links.

Important to our discussion is the structure of the amino acids. These compounds resemble glucose and its intermediary breakdown products, but each amino acid has an ammonia molecule as an integral part; for example, glucose-NH3 is glutamic acid, one of the amino acids.

As if by magic, the body can remove the amino group from the end of the sugar moieties and use the resulting sugar for fuel. The amino group is then excreted as urea. Thus the protein in the muscles serves as a large, secondary fuel depot for the body. (Animals have been demonstrated to form some amino acids when they are fed urea and carbohydrates—so the deamination reaction works both ways. Carbohydrates can, under the proper circumstances, be converted to proteins.)

Unfortunately perhaps, the body would rather deaminate proteins and burn them for fuel than to burn the fat stores. Thus the proteins, both those in the muscles and diet, like carbohydrates, tend to protect the fat stores. This is important for those trying to control their weight. The body jealously guards the fat, burning first the carbohydrates then proteins. This is particularly significant when a plateau is reached in a weight-loss program. The body becomes very adept at deaminating proteins to provide the carbohydrates for its fuel. The no-carbohydrate, high-protein diet that produces an early rapid weight loss fails after about a month because the body learns to supply its carbohydrate needs by deaminating and burning protein.

Meat-eating animals such as lions and tigers depend on this deamination of dietary proteins for their carbohydrate fuel needs. Because there is little carbohydrate in their diets (although they are high in fats), it is difficult for these animals to become obese. Much of their protein is converted to carbohydrate and burned. Their fat is unprotected. Lack of sufficient carbohydrate stores makes it difficult for them to pursue long chases. Their plant-eating prey can outlast them in the chase if they can avoid the initial high-speed pursuit.

When plateauing occurs in a diet program, it may become necessary to reduce protein consumption as well as omitting carbohydrates to continue to lose weight by forcing the body to burn fat.

The knowledge that body fat comes mainly from fat absorbed from the intestine allows another weight-loss short cut. Fat absorption can be greatly reduced by taking calcium carbonate supplements. Calcium will combine with dietary fat and prevent its absorption by turning it into insoluble soap. (This same chemical reaction makes bathtub rings—the calcium in hard water combines with oils from the skin and soap to form the curdy substance that sticks to the sides of the tub.) Calcium supplements with meals are particularly useful in preventing the accumulation of new fat. It will not, however, cause old fat to be burned at an increased rate.

Dr. Gibbons's Quick Weight-Loss Diet

The quick weight-loss diet combined with calcium supplementation forces the body to burn stored fat at a very rapid rate because fat metabolism without carbohydrates is very inefficient and wasteful. This diet is not to be used by persons who are not in otherwise good health.

Calcium carbonate: Take two 500–600 milligram tablets of calcium carbonate with each meal.

The following may be eaten without restrictions as to amount:

salt
pepper
garlic
lemon
mint
mustard
parsley
nutmeg
vanilla
cinnamon
celery salt
vinegar

Vegetables: You may eat unrestricted amounts of the following raw. Limit cooked vegetables to one cup.

asparagus
lettuce
broccoli
mushrooms
cabbage
peppers (green or red)
cauliflower
radishes
celery
sauerkraut
cucumbers
squash

eggplant
string beans
greens (beet, chard, collard, kale, spinach, turnip greens)
tomatoes
watercress

Meats: Amounts restricted to the equivalent of three hard-boiled eggs a day.

beef
pork
fish
poultry
eggs
cheese (cheddar, Swiss, cottage, etc.)

Fats: Small amounts. (With fat-containing meals, be sure to take calcium carbonate.)

avocado
bacon
butter or margarine
dressings (French, mayonnaise, Roquefort), cooking
  oils and olives.

Miscellaneous: Unrestricted.

diet soda pop
bouillon
coffee or tea without sugar
sour dill pickles
noncaloric sweeteners
artificially sweetened gelatin desserts

The following should be scrupulously avoided:

All foods containing sugar or starch, including all fruits (except tomatoes), all breads, cakes, crackers, cereals, pasta, milk, candy and sugar-containing soda pop, ice cream, corn, beans, and potatoes.

Conclusion

The purpose of this book is to help those who suffer from irritable bowel disease to discover which foods are responsible for irritating their particular digestive systems. Most individuals with any of the irritable bowel diseases will experience improvement by avoiding fructose, lactose, sorbitol, mannitol, and wheat bran. For most, eliminating these foods will give complete relief from their symptoms. For others, this diet may not be the full answer. Some have peculiar intolerances to specific foods that most others can eat with impunity. For example, some with IBS complain about lettuce. I am unaware of the specific elements in this food that cause symptoms. Others note worsening of their disease after eating chocolate.

The important point here is that each individual must do some detective work to determine which foods are responsible for his or her symptoms. The vast majority will trace their problems to intolerance to the sugars described in this book. Foods that cause gas formation, loose stools, pain, or bloating are to be avoided. The first suspects to be considered are the sugars and wheat bran. All humans are irritated by sorbitol and mannitol. These are to be carefully avoided by everyone with a tendency for irritable bowel diseases.

The diets suggested here are admittedly spartan, but the benefits to your health will make the dietary sacrifices more than worthwhile. The diet may be weak in vitamins, especially vitamin C. It is advisable when on any restricted diet to take a multiple vitamin tablet daily, especially where there is already impaired digestion.

To arrive at a diet compatible with one's digestive system may require that one discard many old notions that have been accepted as fact. The very worst diet is the one that irritates the bowel—no matter what its vitamin and mineral virtues might be. The first goal is to find a diet that does not harm the intestine. Secondarily, one may worry about nutrient values, not the other way about. The irritated bowel does not absorb nutrients well and no matter how nutritious the food might be, unabsorbed nutrients are useless.

The notion that optimum health requires a quart of milk per day must be disregarded by most colitis sufferers. The idea that fiber is important to health must likewise be put aside. Fiber and complex carbohydrates often behave in the same manner as poorly digested sugars in the irritable bowel. The undigested fiber serves as fodder for bacteria and yeasts in the colon. For those with irritable bowel disease, the ideal is to eat carbohydrates that are rapidly converted to glucose and quickly absorbed. Cooking food is the most practical way of "predigesting" foods so this rapid conversion to glucose can occur.

To the students of dietology, striking similarities will be noted between the colitis diet outlined in this book and some others that are currently popular. Dr. William G. Crook's yeast connection diet avoids many carbohydrates—including fructose and lactose. The benefits noted from his diet probably result from the exclusion of these sugars rather than from the program as a whole. The diet alone is probably as effective as the diet plus the antifungal drug. His book *The Yeast Connection* makes many unscientific propositions: One is that complex carbohydrates are good, and refined (simple) carbohydrates are bad. The prescribed diet probably does nothing to reduce yeast proliferation, as yeast grows equally well on complex carbohydrates (yeast grows quite well on sawdust or cardboard!). A second erroneous proposition is that undesirable fermentation in the gastrointestinal tract is mainly due to yeast. There are myriad different microorganisms in the gut. In addition to yeast, many species of bacteria attack and ferment any good substrate that may be available. The anti- yeast diet also recommends the avoidance of raised bakery foods. Although it is true these employ yeast for leavening, baking destroys all of the yeast organisms. In addition, the bread yeasts are quite different from the monilial yeasts discussed in his book. These grow in and on people. Bread yeast never infects humans. When bread spoils, mold—not yeast—attacks it. The yeast-connection diet is beneficial for some people, probably not because of its antiyeast aspect, but because lactose and fructose are not included.

Another similar diet that has proven to be beneficial to some adherents is that of Dr. Collin H. Dong. In his book *Hope for the Arthritic* he recommends a diet high in protein and vegetables and the elimination of dairy products and fruit sugar. The diet professed little scientific basis. It is patterned after the Chinese diet of vegetables, pork, chicken, beef, fish, and rice. (Note the absence of lactose and fructose.)

Arthritis is one of the common complications of IBS. Many people following the colitis diet have noted improvement in their arthritis. Personally, I can detect an immediate aggravation of my mild arthritis upon departure from the diet when significant amounts of fructose have been consumed.

Dr. Dong's diet also avoids red meat. Meat avoidance perhaps reduces uric acid production and may help avoid gout, one cause of arthritis. I fail to see the difference between consuming red meat and poultry, as both produce purine or uric acid. I am convinced this diet helps many with their arthritis, but not for the reasons Dr. Dong says. Instead, it relieves an underlying irritable bowel condition that is causing the arthritis.

These two diets hit on some of the right combinations empirically rather than with sound chemical principles in mind. The Dong diet does recognize lactose intolerance but does not regard it as a primary item, but rather as a problem secondary to problems of the immune system.

The Colitis Conspiracy

Long ago, a famous man said, "The earth is flat." Casual observation seemed to confirm his declaration, and for two thousand years, the earth was flat because he had said so. There were of course, observations that seemed to indicate otherwise, but no one dared challenge the notion because he was a very great man. This false concept stalled the advance of scientific knowledge for ages.

This same flat-earth mentality exists today in many fields of science including medicine. Many ideas that have become articles of faith of allopathic (orthodox) modern medicine are based on "the earth is flat" concepts. And so long as specialists profit from and prescribe treatments that make a condition such as colitis worse, there will be no hope for recovery. The cause has to be eliminated.

Several years ago, I joined a medical group in the Washington D.C. area. As a junior partner of the group, I was assigned to follow the group's hospitalized patients. This, however, allowed me to try the theory of fructose intolerance I had developed while grappling with my own colitis.

All of the thirty-two colitis patients I had occasion to treat improved dramatically. I made an important discovery in the treatment of a "lifelong, incurable" disease.

Patients with ulcerative colitis, IBS, and Crohn's disease improved spectacularly when fructose and lactose sugars were removed from their diets.

Dr. Ray was a gastroenterologist practicing at our hospital. When our group needed to refer patients with gastrointestinal problems, we sent them to Dr. Ray. Seeing spectacular success with my dietary treatment of these colitis patients, I approached him. "Dr. Ray, I think I have discovered a much better way to treat ulcerative colitis and Crohn's. Would you have a dozen cases that are not improving we could try it on?"

"Listen, De," he said, "I have a wife and kids to feed. These patients come in faithfully each week. They pay for my services. If you have a cure—I don't want to hear about it." He then walked off. (Beware, this could be your doctor!)

This attitude is not uncommon in medicine. Consider the consequences of the discovery of a shot or pill that would cure colitis. Established practices and treatments would change radically. Internists and gastroenterologists would lose their money-making routines and have to learn new methods.

Thinking I had made an important discovery for colitis sufferers (which I had), I called to inform the Colitis Crohn's Foundation of America at their offices in New York City. I was curtly informed that they were not interested in any cures and asked to please not bother them anymore. It took a little while to realize why they were so arrogant and not interested in a cure—the status quo would change and some would lose their jobs and retirement plans. The earth must remain flat so long as the livelihoods of some depend on it. (Beware, this could be your support group!)

Soon after joining the editorial staff of the *Saturday Evening Post* in 1984, I proposed starting a Colitis Club to the editor. I assured her we could help a great number of her readers by offering a diet based on my experience with irritable bowel disease, the diet you have just been reading about.

Thirty thousand people wrote in for copies of the diet. Along with the diets we sent out, we included a questionnaire. When 2,500 questionnaires had been returned, we were overwhelmed. Ninety-one percent of the respondents indicated substantial improvement in their irritable bowel disease.

The following are typical of the letters we received:

"I thought your diet was a lark but tried it anyway. The bleeding stopped after two weeks, and the diarrhea was gone at the end of the month. Thanks."

"I am a dietitian. I have suffered from ulcerative colitis for twenty years. You correctly diagnosed the cause of my colitis—fructose. I have gone through all my textbooks, the university library, my lecture notes, I could not find a single word on fructose intolerance or it causing colitis. I cannot express my gratitude."

"Thank you so much for sending the colitis diet. Your suggestions on fructose were invaluable. It was like finally putting the puzzle pieces of my health problems together and seeing the whole picture."

I received a phone call from a psychiatrist in Virginia:

"I had to call you and thank you for the information in your diet. I have literally spent a fortune at the Johns Hopkins Medical Center with the Chief of Service. Nothing ever helped my ulcerative colitis until I followed your diet. Thank you, thank you."

There is a de facto conspiracy against you because you have colitis. Much of the health care establishment needs you to remain ill—their livings depend on it. You must take control of your own health and destiny by taking a self-help approach to your IBS.

Index

Page references followed by the letter "f" indicate a figure.